Tom Mayen

Series/Number 07-119

MW00470964

ODDS RATIOS IN THE ANALYSIS OF CONTINGENCY TABLES

TAMÁS RUDAS
*Central European University
and TÁRKI*

SAGE PUBLICATIONS
International Educational and Professional Publisher
Thousand Oaks   London   New Delhi

For information:

 SAGE Publications, Inc.
2455 Teller Road
Thousand Oaks, California 91320
E-mail: order@sagepub.com

SAGE Publications Ltd.
6 Bonhill Street
London EC2A 4PU
United Kingdom

SAGE Publications India Pvt. Ltd.
M-32 Market
Greater Kailash I
New Delhi 110 048 India

Printed in the United States of America

Library of Congress Cataloging-in-Publication Data

Rudas, Tamás.
   Odds ratios in the analysis of contingency tables / Tamás Rudas.
     p. cm. — (Sage university papers series. Quantitative
applications in the social sciences ; no. 07-119)
  Includes bibliographical references (p.).
  ISBN 0-7619-0362-3 (pbk.: acid-free paper)
   1. Contingency tables. 2. Social sciences—Statistical methods.
I. Title. II. Series.
QA277.R84 1998
519.5′37—dc21   97-33790

98 99 00 01 02 03 10 9 8 7 6 5 4 3 2 1

Acquiring Editor:	C. Deborah Laughton
Editorial Assistant:	Eileen Carr
Production Editor:	Michèle Lingre
Production Assistant:	Denise Santoyo
Typesetter:	Rebecca Evans

CONTENTS

SERIES EDITOR'S INTRODUCTION

Social scientific observations are made at different levels of precision. When the data are qualitative, rather than quantitative, the common mode of analysis is tabular. In the **Quantitative Analysis in the Social Sciences** (QASS) series, several papers introduce the researcher to the statistics of contingency tables: *Analysis of Nominal Data* (Reynolds, No. 7), *Analysis of Ordinal Data* (Hildebrand, Laing, & Rosenthal, No. 8), *Measures of Association* (Liebetrau, No. 32), and *Nonparametric Measures of Association* (Gibbons, No. 91). A traditional explication of a simple cross-tab, say a 3×3 for two ordinal variables, might begin with interpretation of differences in cell percentages and end with presentation of an appropriate measure of association, such as tau-b. Another strain of contingency table work pursues log-linear modeling. Instead of a table of percentages, the researcher may begin with a table of raw frequencies, to be converted into odds and compared in an *odds ratio*. Log-linear modeling can become quite sophisticated. Fortunately, the QASS series has a number of relevant papers: *Log-Linear Models* (Knoke & Burke, No. 20), *Logit Modeling* (DeMaris, No. 86), *Loglinear Models With Latent Variables* (Hagenaars, No. 94), *Ordinal Log-Linear Models* (Ishii-Kuntz, No. 97), and *Interpreting Probability Models* (Liao, No. 101).

In the current monograph, Professor Rudas uses odds ratios as a framework for the understanding of log-linear models. He carefully defines the odds ratio and shows how it is a measure of association for tabular analysis. The text is tightly organized, moving systematically from the paradigmatic 2×2 case to more complicated tables. Real examples are regularly provided from the famous Stouffer data on American soldiers in World War II. The data set is well chosen, for it allows hypotheses of intuitive appeal to be tested on a very large sample. His first tables suggest the utility of the odds ratio as a measure of association. Does present army camp location (North vs. South) relate to preferred army camp location (North vs. South)? For soldiers presently in the North, the odds of perferring a Northern camp are 2.84, but for soldiers presently in the South, the odds of preferring a Northern camp are only .67 (calculated from the raw frequencies in

Table 1.2). Present camp location makes a difference for camp preference. How strong is that relationship? An answer to that question comes from consideration of the ratio of these odds: 2.84/.67 = 4.27. This odds ratio says that soldiers already in the North are more than four times as likely to prefer a camp in the North as soldiers in the South are. Present camp location appears to have at least a moderate effect on camp preference.

To assess the magnitude of any measure of association, it is helpful to know how it is bounded. The odds ratio takes on only positive values and is 1.0 when there is no relationship. It has no upper bound. It can still be used comparatively because of its direct interpretation. For example, from the above data, when the independent variable is birthplace (North vs. South) rather than current camp location, the odds ratio is 10.19. A comparison of the two odds ratios—4.27 and 10.19—indicates that birthplace clearly is more important than current location for explaining preference.

Odds ratios can be generalized to larger tables. One way is by "local odds ratios," and another way is by the "spanning cell approach." Both are explicated here. Professor Rudas goes on to demonstrate that they yield desirable statistical properties. Odds ratios also can be generalized to tables of higher dimension, giving a conditional odds ratio. For example, one could look at the odds ratio of the above location and preference variables, conditional on the region of birth (see Table 3.1). Furthermore, conditional odds ratios can be broadened to polytomous variables.

Traditionally, the measures of association called on for contingency table analysis are single, summary correlation-type coefficients; such as gamma, tau-b, and lambda. Professor Rudas convinces us, among other things, of the value of an alternative—the odds ratios—that is, as he rightly observes, a natural measure of association.

—*Michael S. Lewis-Beck*
Series Editor

ODDS RATIOS IN THE ANALYSIS OF CONTINGENCY TABLES

TAMÁS RUDAS
Central European University and TÁRKI

INTRODUCTION

One of the most important developments in social science methodology during the last 30 years is the growing use of categorical data analysis methods. Many of the data available in the social sciences have always been categorical but, for a number of reasons, for a long period of time, appropriate methods were not present or, at least, were not generally used. This importance is well reflected in the series **Quantitative Applications in the Social Sciences** (QASS). Of the more than 100 titles available in the series, 11 deal primarily with categorical or ordinal data analysis, and at least in five further volumes categorical data play an important role.

Log-linear, generalized log-linear, row-column, and other association models, and logistic regression are all well known to social scientists. Careful application of these methods provides the researcher with very flexible tools to model the structure of the population underlying the data. The purpose of this monograph is not to introduce new models for categorical data analysis but rather to present these and other models in a unified framework. I not only will show how these models are related but also will provide additional interpretations not usually emphasized in textbooks.

The presentation in this book is centered around *odds ratios*. Relationships among variables are often more interesting than the variables themselves, and I will argue that these relationships, as long as the variables are categorical or ordinal, are best captured by odds ratios. Furthermore, all techniques referred to above analyze the associations by analyzing odds ratios.

Titles in the *QASS* series directly relevant to the topic of this book include Reynolds (No. 7, 1984), Knoke and Burke (No. 20, 1980), De-Maris (No. 86, 1992), Hagenaars (No. 94, 1993), Ishii-Kuntz (No. 97, 1994), and Liao (No. 101, 1994). Reynolds (1984) contains the standard notation and describes some of the traditional methods for the analysis of nominal data, and the other volumes describe special techniques and models. These models, as well as those in Clogg and Shihadeh (1994), will be discussed in this book but the coverage here is, of course, much less detailed. For those who are already familiar with the contents of these books, this one offers an overview and summary by emphasizing the common underlying concepts. For those readers who are beginning their studies in contingency table analysis methods with this book, the material here will be helpful for understanding the essence of some of the most popular methods; studying more detailed accounts, like the ones referred to above, then will be easier and more effective.

I am indebted to many of my students for their comments on the material in this book and especially to Attila Seress for drawing my attention to several errors in earlier versions of the manuscript.

1. THE ODDS RATIO IN 2 × 2 TABLES

This chapter summarizes the most important properties of the odds ratio in 2 × 2 tables with emphasis given to those properties that will be preserved in more general forms. Section A defines and describes the odds ratio as a measure of association among the variables forming the table. Section B extends the discussion with the introduction and illustration of one of the most remarkable properties of the odds ratio: It is variation independent of the marginals. That is, any pair of marginal distributions can be combined with any possible value of the odds ratio. The odds ratio therefore is a parameter of the distribution in the contingency table that is not affected by the marginal distributions and depends on the *association* among the variables only. Section C describes the log-linear representation for a 2 × 2 table, shows how independence of the marginals of the table is related to a special kind of log-linear representation, and describes the relationship between the odds ratio and the log-linear interaction term.

A. The Odds Ratio as a Measure of Association

Association is one of the most important themes in statistical data analysis in the social sciences. This is true in part because social scientists do not usually stop their analyses at estimating fractions of the population belonging to the respective categories of a variable. Rather, they tend to

TABLE 1.1

Preferred Camp Location of
World War II American Soldiers

Preference	
North	*South*
4051	3985

SOURCE: Stouffer, Suchmann, Devinney, Star, &
Williams (1949).

ask why. Why is 20% of the population in one category and 30% in another
one? If more people in one country belong to the second category, why is
it that more people in another country belong to the first category? Depending on the context, there may be several ways to answer these questions.
One of the most general approaches is to describe the people in the
respective categories of the variable of interest in terms of other variables.
These other variables may include, for example, gender, educational level,
socioeconomic status, age, or political party preference. When information
regarding any of these or other variables "helps to explain" what happens
with the variable of interest, we say that there is association among the
variables.

Depending on the *levels of measurement* of the variables involved, the
general approach described above may take various forms. For example,
when all the variables are measured on a ratio scale, *regression analysis* is
the usual formulation. With variables measured at other levels, the same
idea leads to techniques known as *discriminant analysis, analysis of
variance,* or *logistic regression.* The same approach also can be applied
when all the variables are measured on a nominal or ordinal scale. In this
case, however, "helps to explain" must be given a meaning specific to these
levels of measurement.

To illustrate the above ideas, I will use data published by Stouffer,
Suchmann, Devinney, Star, and Williams (1949) and subsequently ana-
lyzed by Goodman (1972), Bishop, Fienberg, and Holland (1975), and
Rudas (1991). The data consist of the responses of 8,036 World War II
American soldiers to a question regarding their preferred camp location.
Like many authors before, I use the data here in a binary (or dichotomous)
form, with the two categories being North and South.

The data in Table 1.1 show that approximately the same number of
soldiers prefer camps in the North and camps in the South. One way of
summarizing the figures in Table 1.1 is to say that 50.4% of the soldiers

preferred a camp in the North and 49.6% preferred a camp in the South, or the odds that a randomly selected soldier preferred a camp in the North, as opposed to a camp in the South, are about 1.02 (= 4,051/3,985).

I do not want to consider here the problem of whether the sample values can be considered reasonable estimates of the relevant population quantities. This is certainly one of the most important questions in statistics and, for the interested reader, I mention only that all quantities in this book, when computed from a sample, are maximum likelihood estimates (see Eliason, 1993) of the underlying population parameters. This assures good properties of these estimators, under certain regularity assumptions and for large samples. The main goal of the present book is to deal with structural issues that apply equally to sample estimates and population parameters.

What is more important for our purposes here is to raise the following questions: whether the above finding remains true (in any approximate sense) for soldiers who originated from the North and for soldiers who originated from the South, whether taking into consideration the location of the present camps of the soldiers would change the odds, and whether the same result applies to black and white soldiers equally. All these questions address the association between the response variable (location of preferred camp) and some other possible explanatory variable.

Tables 1.2, 1.3, and 1.4, which help to answer the above questions, are cross-classifications of the respondents according to the response variable and the potential explanatory variables referred to above. Although the overall finding was that approximately the same number of soldiers preferred a camp in the North as in the South, things look quite different for those whose present camp is in the North as compared with those whose present camp is in the South. As can be easily calculated from the data in Table 1.2, the odds in favor of a camp in the North are 2.84 (= 1,829/644) for the first group and 0.67 (= 2,222/3,341) for the second. There appears to be a tendency to prefer a camp in the same part of the country (North or South) where the present camp is. Note that this approach does not distinguish between soldiers who would prefer to stay in their present camp and soldiers who prefer to move to another camp in the same region. Because the odds for the two groups of soldiers (whose present camps are in the North versus those whose present camps are in the South) were different, the data show that there is association among the variables Preference and Location.

A similar analysis of the data in Table 1.3 reveals that the odds of preferring a camp in the North as opposed to a camp in the South are 3.23 for those whose region of origin is the North and 0.32 for those whose

TABLE 1.2

Preferred Camp Location of World War II American Soldiers
Cross-Classified by Location of the Present Camp

	Preference	
Location	North	South
North	1,829	644
South	2,222	3,341

SOURCE: Stouffer et al. (1949).

TABLE 1.3

Preferred Camp Location of World War II American Soldiers
Cross-Classified by Region of Origin of the Soldier

	Preference	
Region of Origin	North	South
North	3,092	958
South	959	3,027

SOURCE: Stouffer et al. (1949).

TABLE 1.4

Preferred Camp Location of World War II American Soldiers
Cross-Classified by Race of the Soldier

	Preference	
Race	North	South
Black	2,027	2,268
White	2,024	1,717

SOURCE: Stouffer et al. (1949).

region of origin is the South. Again, because these odds differ considerably, one can conclude that there is association between the region of origin and the preferred camp location. The soldiers tend to prefer a camp in the same part of the country (North or South) where they are presently located and also in the region from which they originated. Because the preferred camp location of a soldier cannot influence his region of origin, and because it is very unlikely that it could influence his present camp location, these associations can be interpreted as Region and Location both having an effect on Preference. Two very important questions suggest themselves at this point: First, if both of these effects are present, which is stronger? Second, how are the two effects related to each other? The second question will be dealt with in Chapter 3, where the first step will be to formulate the question more precisely.

One way to quantify the strength of association is to compute the *odds ratio,* which is the ratio of the two odds considered above. For the association between Location and Preference, the value of 4.27 (= 2.84/0.67) is obtained. This quantity shows how many times more likely a camp in the North will be preferred (as opposed to a camp in the South) for a soldier whose present camp is in the North as compared with a soldier whose present camp is in the South. If one adopts the usual notation of denoting the frequencies in a 2×2 table with f_{11} and f_{12} in the first row and by f_{21} and f_{22} in the second row, the odds ratio is

$$\frac{f_{11} f_{22}}{f_{12} f_{21}} \qquad [1.1]$$

This formula also leads us to the value of 4.27 for the odds ratio. The quantity in Equation 1.1 is sometimes referred to as the *cross product ratio.* Note that the odds ratio in Equation 1.1 is equal not only to the ratio of the odds f_{11}/f_{12} and f_{21}/f_{22} but also to the ratio of the odds f_{11}/f_{21} and f_{12}/f_{22} .

For the data in Table 1.3, the odds ratio is 10.19, which means that the odds of preferring a Northern camp are 10.19 times greater for those who come from the North than for those who come from the South. This shows stronger association between Region and Preference than between Location and Preference.

The value of the odds ratio for the data in Table 1.4 is 0.76, which shows that black soldiers do not prefer camps in the North versus camps in the South as much as white soldiers do. This is a correct interpretation because the value of the odds ratio is less than one, implying that the odds of preferring a camp in the North, as opposed to a camp in the South, are smaller for black soldiers than for white soldiers. In fact, black soldiers appear to prefer camps in the South, which is indicated by the relevant odds being less than 1, namely 0.89 (= 2,027/2,268). On the other hand, the same odds for white soldiers are greater than 1, namely 1.18 (= 2,024/1,717), showing that they prefer camps in the North. Note that the odds ratio can be less than or greater than one, irrespective of whether or not the odds themselves are less than or greater than one. The odds measure the strength of preference in the respective categories, and the odds ratio compares these strengths.

When, in the data available, one or both of the frequencies f_{12} and f_{21} are zero, the *observed* odds ratio cannot be computed. Using an appropriate *statistical model*—that is, assumptions about the underlying population—it may still be possible to estimate the odds ratio in the population. The same considerations then apply to the table of estimated probabilities and the table of estimated frequencies. The odds ratios computed from a table of frequencies and from the table of corresponding probabilities are the same because the division or multiplication of all entries by the sample size cancels out from the formula for the odds ratio.

When all the entries in the table are positive, the odds ratio can take on any positive value. If the odds ratio is equal to 1, there is said to be no association between the variables because, in this case, the two odds that are compared in the odds ratio are equal. The farther from 1 is the value is, the stronger the association. For example, the values of 0.25 and 4 are equally distant from 1 because $0.25 = 1/4$. These values therefore refer to the same strength of association. Sometimes direction can be attributed to the association. This can be done by taking into account the ordering of the categories of variables in the table and by determining whether or not the odds ratio is greater than or less than one. When the ordering of the categories of one variable is reversed, the odds ratio will change to its reciprocal (i.e., for example, from 4 to 0.25). When the order of the categories of the other variable is also reversed, the odds ratio will change to its reciprocial again (i.e., from 0.25 back to 4).

A value and its reciprocial therefore refer not just to the *same strength of association* but also to the *same association,* unless the categories of the two variables have fixed orderings with respect to each other. This can happen if both variables are ordinal; in this case, one can order the categories of both variables in increasing order or both in decreasing order. Either way, the value of the odds ratio remains the same. For example, in an educational mobility table, with categories "low" and "high," the educational attainment of both father and son should be ordered the same way. The value of the odds ratio will be the same under both possible orderings. Thus, whether the value is above or below unity is informative. This is true not only for ordinal variables but also for categorical variables, supposing the two variables have the same categories. For example, in Table 1.2, as long as the categories North and South have the same ordering for both variables, the odds ratio will tell whether a location in the North makes it more or less likely to prefer a camp in the North. In the first case the association is positive, and in the second it is negative. A similar interpretation is impossible for the data in Table 1.4 because the categories are unrelated.

The odds ratio is equal to 1 if and only if the two variables are independent in the table. In this case, the odds computed separately in the categories of one variable, for the comparison of the two categories of the other variable, are equal. Moreover, they are also equal to the *marginal odds,* that is, the odds computed from the marginal distribution. For example, the odds in Table 1.2 (2.84 and 0.67) are different. These odds may be called *conditional odds,* for they show the odds of preferring a camp in the North as opposed to a camp in the South, computed under the *condition* that the respondents only in one category of the other variable are taken into account. These conditional odds are different from each other as well as from the marginal odds that can be computed from Table 1.1 (1.02).

B. Variation Independence of the Odds Ratio and the Marginals

The odds ratio was introduced in the previous section as a measure of association. This was done without any clear definition of what was meant by association. In fact, association was defined *via* the odds ratio. There are several other ways to measure the association between two binary variables, but it is more precise to say that these different measures actually measure different aspects of association. To highlight a highly desirable property of the odds ratio as a measure of association (or, more precisely, a desirable property of the definition of association related to the odds ratio), I introduce another measure of association. This is the ratio of the frequency (or probability) in cell $(1, 1)$ to what would be expected if the two variables were independent:

$$\frac{nf_{11}}{f_{1+}f_{+1}} = \frac{p_{11}}{p_{1+}p_{+1}} \qquad [1.2]$$

where n is the number of observations, each f is an observed frequency, each p is an observed probability, and subscripts indicate rows and columns, with a + indicating a marginal. The measure of association in Equation 1.2 shows how many times more likely it is to have an observation in cell $(1, 1)$ than it would be to have one under independence. A value close to one indicates a weak relationship. Note that a value of Equation 1.2 close to unity implies the same for all three of the other cells of the table.

The measure of association in Equation 1.2 is not suitable for every purpose. Suppose, for example, that the value of the formula in Equation

TABLE 1.5
Two Sets of Data With the Same Value
From Equation 1.2

18	27		18	12
2	53		12	58

1.2 is 2. Is this a strong association or not? To answer this, consider the two sets of data in Table 1.5.

In both sets of data there are 100 observations, and in both cases the product of the first row marginal and the first column marginal is 900. Therefore, under independence, the expected frequency in cell (1, 1) is 9 for both, yielding the value of 2 in Equation 1.2. In both cases, the frequency in cell (1, 1) is twice as much as would be expected under independence. For the first table, given the marginals, the frequency in cell (1, 1) could not be much greater than 18 because the first column total is 20. The maximum possible value of the frequency in cell (1, 1) therefore is 20, which would give a value of 2.22 from Equation 1.2. Given the marginals, the association as measured by Equation 1.2 is close to its maximum. For the second set of data, on the other hand, the value of 2 is far from the maximum possible value of Equation 1.2, which, given the marginals, is 3.33 (= 30/9).

The association in the first set of data, in the above sense, is stronger than the association in the second set of data because it is closer to its possible maximum. Therefore, given the marginals, the value of 2 for the quantity in Equation 1.2 means a stronger association for the first set of data than for the second. Note that the odds ratios for the data are 17.67 for the first set and 7.25 for the second set, supporting the above claim.

The difficulty with the quantity in Equation 1.2, as illustrated in the above numerical example, is that the range of possible values is influenced by the marginal distributions of the variables, even though one would believe that the strength of association should depend only on the *joint distribution* of the variables and should not depend on the marginal distributions. Whatever the marginal distributions of the variables are, the strength of the association among them may be arbitrarily small or arbitrarily large, depending on their joint distribution. In fact, one qualitative definition of *association* is that it is the information in the joint distribution (i.e., in the contingency table) not contained in the marginal distributions.

The most appealing property of the odds ratio as a measure of association is that its possible range of values is not influenced by the marginal distributions of the variables involved. A more precise formulation of this property is as follows. For a 2×2 table, the marginal probabilities p_{1+} (first row marginal) and p_{+1} (first column marginal) are chosen arbitrarily, but strictly between 0 and 1, and an arbitrary positive α is chosen for the value of the odds ratio. There always exists exactly one 2×2 table of probabilities with the given marginals and odds ratio. In other words, the marginals and the odds ratio can vary independently from each other, which is called *variation independence*. Yet another formulation of this variation independence is that if one arbitrarily selects two 2×2 tables with positive entries, then there always exists a third 2×2 table in which the marginal distributions are as they were in the first table and the odds ratio is as it was in the second table. Therefore, the odds ratio measures a property of the 2×2 distribution that is not influenced by the marginals, and this is exactly the association.

The variation independence property described above should be distinguished clearly from another independence property often encountered in this book: the independence of the two variables forming the table. This latter independence is sometimes referred to as *stochastic independence*. Stochastic independence is a possible property of the joint distribution of the variables, that is, of the contingency table. Variation independence is a property of a parameterization of this joint distribution. This parameterization is based on the two marginal probabilities and the odds ratio.

Note that the two marginal probabilities p_{1+} and p_{+1} are also variation independent in that they can be selected independently from each other. Variation independence is a property not shared by most other parameterizations of the distribution in the table. Natural, and therefore very appealing, parameterizations are not usually variation independent. For example, it appears to be natural to use the three cell probabilities p_{11}, p_{12}, and p_{21} to describe the distribution. If the value of p_{11} has been selected, it restricts the possible range of p_{12} (because $p_{12} \leq 1 - p_{11}$ follows). If $p_{11} = 0.3$, then p_{12} is less than or equal to 0.7, which makes $p_{12} = 0.8$ impossible. Similarly, once p_{11} and p_{12} have been selected, the possible range of p_{21} is influenced. These are not variation independent parameters for the distribution in the 2×2 table because they do not reflect distinct pieces of information.

The remainder of this section will show how a table that combines arbitrary marginal distributions with an arbitrary odds ratio can be obtained. This is based on a procedure called iterative proportional fitting. A

TABLE 1.6

Starting Table for Iterative Proportional Fitting
With the Odds Ratio Equal to 2/3

2/11	3/11
3/11	3/11

TABLE 1.7

The First Step of Iterative Proportional Fitting

$\dfrac{2}{11} * \dfrac{44}{50} = \dfrac{4}{25}$	$\dfrac{3}{11} * \dfrac{44}{50} = \dfrac{6}{25}$
$\dfrac{3}{11} * \dfrac{11}{10} = \dfrac{3}{10}$	$\dfrac{3}{11} * \dfrac{11}{10} = \dfrac{3}{10}$

detailed analysis of the properties of this procedure is, however, outside the scope of the present book. The interested reader can consult standard references such as Bishop and colleagues (1975) or Agresti (1990).

Suppose, for example, that the prescribed marginal probabilities are $p_{1+} = 0.4$ and $p_{+1} = 0.3$ and the odds ratio is 2/3. The procedure starts with a 2×2 table in which the odds ratio is equal to 2/3. Table 1.6 has this property.

The row marginals here are $p_{1+} = 5/11$ and $p_{2+} = 6/11$. These are the actual marginals. The desired marginals are $p_{1+} = 0.4$ and $p_{2+} = 0.6$. In the first step of the procedure, every cell probability is multiplied by the ratio of the desired row marginal and the actual row marginal. The probabilities in the first row are multiplied by $(4/10)/(5/11) = 44/50$ and the probabilities in the second row are multiplied by $(6/10)/(6/11) = 11/10$. This leads to Table 1.7.

Note that the transformation of Table 1.6 that led to Table 1.7 did not change the value of the odds ratio. This is because both the numerator and the denominator were multiplied by the same numbers. We also see that the row marginals are as desired but the column marginals are not yet equal to what they should be. The actual column marginals are $p_{+1} = 23/50$ and $p_{+2} = 27/50$, and the desired column marginals are $p_{+1} = 0.3$ and $p_{+2} = 0.7$. Again, every cell probability is multiplied by the ratio of the desired and actual values of the relevant column marginal. Probabilities in the first column are multiplied by $(3/10)/(23/50) = 15/23$, and probabilities in the second column are multiplied by $(7/10)/(27/50) = 35/27$. These multiplications are performed in Table 1.8.

TABLE 1.8
The Second Step of Iterative Proportional Fitting

$\dfrac{4}{25} * \dfrac{15}{23} = \dfrac{12}{115}$	$\dfrac{6}{25} * \dfrac{35}{27} = \dfrac{14}{45}$
$\dfrac{3}{10} * \dfrac{15}{23} = \dfrac{9}{46}$	$\dfrac{3}{10} * \dfrac{35}{27} = \dfrac{7}{18}$

TABLE 1.9
The Third Step of Iterative Proportional Fitting

$\dfrac{12}{115} * \dfrac{207}{215} = \dfrac{108}{1,075}$	$\dfrac{14}{45} * \dfrac{207}{215} = \dfrac{322}{1,075}$
$\dfrac{9}{46} * \dfrac{621}{605} = \dfrac{243}{1,210}$	$\dfrac{7}{18} * \dfrac{621}{605} = \dfrac{483}{1,210}$

The transformation also did not change the value of the odds ratio, and the column marginals are as desired. The row marginals, however, did change and are not equal to the desired values. A similar step to the first one therefore will be performed in which every cell probability is multiplied by the ratio of the desired row marginal probability to the actual row marginal probability. Cell probabilities in the first row are multiplied by $(4/10)/(86/207) = 207/215$ and the in the second row by $(6/10)/(121/207) = 621/605$. This leads to the data given in Table 1.9.

In this table, the odds ratio and the row marginals are as desired, but the column marginals need to be changed. The next step of the iteration is similar to the second step, as it adjusts the column marginals. After this, a step similar to the first step, or to the third step, is performed. These two kinds of steps (row and column adjustments) are applied one after the other. After a number of steps are performed, changes in the later steps will affect the probabilities very little. The longer one continues this procedure, the smaller the changes will be: The iteration converges. In this example, the results are given in Table 1.10, which has all the desired properties.

Note that the numerical values of the entries in Table 1.9 are equal to the theoretical values given in Table 1.10 for three digits after the decimal. In other words, with a precision of 0.001, convergence has occurred.

An interesting property of the iterative proportional fitting procedure is that when the odds ratio is chosen to be equal to 1, the iteration stops after the first two steps. In this case, the adjustment of the column marginals does not change the row marginals.

TABLE 1.10

The Result of Iterative Proportional Fitting

0.1	0.3
0.2	0.4

C. Log-Linear Representation of the Cell Probabilities

This section will describe the log-linear representation for a 2×2 table. This representation can be extended naturally to higher dimensional tables and leads to log-linear models, which are the most important tools for contingency table analysis. It will be shown that the log-linear representation is a parameterization of the cell probabilities that is closely related to the parameterization by marginal probabilities and the odds ratio and that shares many of its desirable properties.

The log-linear representation is a parameterization of the logarithm of the cell probabilities (or of the cell frequencies) in terms of additive effects. The logarithm applied here is the natural logarithm (base e), but any other logarithm could do as well. In the log-linear representation, separate additive effects pertain to the marginal distributions and to the association among the variables. A symbolic form of the log-linear representation is *logarithm of the cell probability = general effect + row effect + column effect + interaction effect*. A similar representation applies to the cell frequencies. Here, the term *row effect* refers to the information related to the differences in the rows, *column effect* refers to the information related to the differences in the columns, and the *interaction effect* refers to the information related to the association among the variables. Although decomposition of information into the above pieces seems to be the right thing to do, the choice of additive representation of the logarithms may appear to be somewhat unnatural. Justifications of this approach include similarity with analysis of variance (Bishop et al., 1975) and information theoretical considerations (Gokhale & Kullback, 1978). The justification offered in this book is that this approach leads to variation independent parameterization closely related to the odds ratio.

An additive representation of the logarithms of the cell probabilities leads to a multiplicative representation of the probabilities as the product of the exponentials of the above terms. To highlight the important properties of the log-linear or the related multiplicative representation, I start with a similar decomposition of the information in the table, which may appear to be more natural but fails on an important point.

When the value of the odds ratio in the actual table is not known, there are several tables with the given marginals, but only one of them has the correct value of the odds ratio and only one of them is independent. As a reference distribution from among these, it appears to be natural to choose the independent one. In this independent distribution, the association is equal to its null value. This null value, as measured by the odds ratio, is one. The value of the odds ratio in the distribution shows how many times greater the association is than its null value.

The value of the odds ratio measures the departure from the reference distribution that is independent and has the same marginal distributions as the actual table of probabilities. (The cell probabilities in this reference distribution are the products of the given marginal probabilities.)

The independent distribution with the given marginals contains a part of the information that is given in the table of probabilities: the marginal distributions. If one continues to remove information successively, the next reference distribution may be the one that contains the information regarding one marginal distribution, say the row marginal, but does not contain the information pertaining to the other marginal, which is replaced by a uniform distribution. The choice of the uniform marginal as reference is supported by the fact that the odds in a uniform distribution (both probabilities being equal to 0.5) are equal to one, which is the null value of the odds.

When the information pertaining to the other marginal distribution, say row marginal, is removed, an independent distribution is left, and both marginals are uniform. Such a distribution is uniform, each cell having a probability of 0.25.

The same decomposition of information can be applied to a table of frequencies. This decomposition of the data in Table 1.2 is given in Table 1.11.

The decomposition in Table 1.11 can be summarized by starting with Table 1.11.a, then multiplying every cell frequency by a number in such a way that one obtains the data in Table 1.11.b. This multiplier reflects the multiplicative effect of rows, because, after the application of this multiplier, the row marginal becomes the same as in the original table. This multiplier is the same for the two cells in the first row: $2,473/4,018 = 0.616$. The multiplier is also the same for the two cells in the second row: $5,563/4,018 = 1.385$. These multipliers are, again, obtained by the rule, "desired marginal divided by actual marginal." Applying the row effect multiplier gives Table 1.11.b. The multiplier representing the column effect can be obtained by dividing the original column marginals by the column marginals of Table 1.11.a or of Table 1.11.b. This gives $4,051/4,018 = 1.008$

TABLE 1.11
Structural Decomposition of the Information in Table 1.2

a. Uniform Distribution

	Preference	
Location	North	South
North	2009	2009
South	2009	2009

b. Row Marginals Restored

	Preference	
Location	North	South
North	1236.5	1236.5
South	2781.5	2781.5

c. Row and Column
Marginals Restored (Independence)

	Preference	
Location	North	South
North	1246.66	1226.34
South	2804.34	2758.66

TABLE 1.12
A Multiplicative Representation of the Data in Table 1.2

	Preference	
Location	North	South
North	2,009 ∗ 0.616 ∗ 1.008 ∗ 1.469	2,009 ∗ 0.616 ∗ 0.992 ∗ 0.525
South	2,009 ∗ 1.385 ∗ 1.008 ∗ 0.792	2,009 ∗ 1.385 ∗ 0.992 ∗ 1.121

for the cells in the first column and $3,985/4,018 = 0.992$ for the cells in the second column. Multiplying in every cell yields Table 1.11.c. Finally, the last multiplier in every cell, namely the ratio of the entry in Table 1.2 to the entry in Table 1.11.c, reflects association. This leads to the decomposition in Table 1.12.

In the above structural representation, the first parameter is the same in every cell, the second parameter (row effect) is the same within rows, and the third parameter (column effect) is the same within columns. The inclusion of an interaction term, finally, yields the original frequencies.

The main reason the structural representation, or decomposition, described above is not used is that the parameter pertaining to interaction, or association, is exactly the quantity in Equation 1.2; therefore, the parameters involved are not variation independent.

The log-linear representation implements the main ideas outlined above and leads to variation independent decomposition of the effects in the table. This starts with the choice of a reference distribution, which will be taken as the uniform distribution. Another possible choice of the reference distribution will be discussed later. The choice of the uniform distribution as reference is justified by the fact that, without knowledge regarding the distribution, one would assign equal chances to an observation belonging to any of the categories. In a log-linear representation, the constant term is the average of the logarithms of the cell frequencies (or cell probabilities). This quantity is usually denoted by λ. Its value for the data in Table 1.2 is $\lambda = 7.450$. The row effect associated with the first row is the average of the logarithms of the cell frequencies (or probabilities) in the first row minus the value of λ. This quantity is usually denoted by λ_1^L, its value being -0.460. Similarly, the value of the parameter associated with the row effect in the second row is the average of the logarithms of the cell frequencies (or probabilities) in the second row minus λ, which is $\lambda_2^L = 0.460$ for the data in Table 1.2. Here the indices 1 and 2 refer to the first and second categories of the variable Location, respectively. It follows directly from the definition that

$$\lambda_1^L + \lambda_2^L = 0 \qquad [1.3]$$

The parameters associated with the column effect are defined similarly. λ_1^P is the average of the logarithms of the cell frequencies in the first column minus λ. For the data in Table 1.2, $\lambda_1^P = 0.159$ and $\lambda_2^P = -0.159$. Thus, a relationship similar to Equation 1.3 holds again.

The parameter related to the association among the variables, the interaction term, denoted for cell (i, j) by λ_{ij}^{LP}, is defined in such a way that the sum of the parameters is equal to the logarithm of the cell frequency (or probability). That is,

$$\lambda_{ij}^{LP} = \log(f_{ij}) - \lambda - \lambda_i^L - \lambda_j^P \qquad [1.4]$$

TABLE 1.13
Log-linear Representation of the Data in Table 1.2

Location	Preference	
	North	South
North	7.450 − 0.460 + 0.159 + 0.366	7.450 − 0.460 − 0.159 − 0.366
South	7.450 + 0.460 + 0.159 − 0.366	7.450 + 0.460 − 0.159 + 0.366

TABLE 1.14
Multiplicative Representation of the Data in Table 1.2
Associated With the Log-linear Parameters

Location	Preference	
	North	South
North	1,719.863 * 0.631 * 1.172 * 1.438	1,719.863 * 0.631 * 0.853 * 0.696
South	1,719.863 * 1.584 * 1.172 * 0.696	1,719.863 * 1.584 * 0.853 * 1.438

For the data in Table 1.2, $\lambda_{11}^{LP} = 0.366$, $\lambda_{12}^{LP} = -0.366$, $\lambda_{21}^{LP} = 0.366$, and $\lambda_{22}^{LP} = -0.366$. For the interaction term, a relationship similar to Equation 1.3 holds:

$$\lambda_{11}^{LP} + \lambda_{12}^{LP} = \lambda_{21}^{LP} + \lambda_{22}^{LP} = \lambda_{11}^{LP} + \lambda_{21}^{LP} = \lambda_{12}^{LP} + \lambda_{22}^{LP} = 0 \qquad [1.5]$$

One way to summarize Equation 1.5, is that the interaction parameter summed in any of its indices is zero.

The log-linear representation for the data in Table 1.2 is given in Table 1.13. The sum of the entries in every cell is equal to the logarithm of the appropriate frequency. The decomposition in Table 1.13 can be compared to the representation in Table 1.12. This can be done by exponentiating all the entries, leading to the following formula: $f_{ij} = e^{\lambda} e^{\lambda_i^L} e^{\lambda_j^P} e^{\lambda_{ij}^{LP}}$. These figures are given in Table 1.14.

A comparison of the numbers in Table 1.14 with the numbers in Table 1.12 reveals that the two decompositions, although both based on the general idea of row effect plus column effect plus association effect, are somewhat different. For example, the decomposition in Table 1.12 suggests a weaker column effect than in Table 1.14 because the multipliers associated with different columns—1.008 versus 0.992—cause smaller differences in

Table 1.12 than the multipliers in Table 1.14—1.169 versus 0.856. More-over, the decomposition related to the the log-linear representation (Table 1.14) suggests that interaction has the same strength in cells (1, 1) and (2, 2) whereas the other representation (Table 1.12) suggests that the association is stronger in cell (1, 1) than in cell (2, 2). Which of these results can be considered valid? The major advantage of the decomposition associated with the log-linear representation is—and this suggests using the log-linear approach—that here the marginal effects are variation independent from the interaction effect; therefore, these parameters are valid measurements of the appropriate effects. In the other representation, the effects cannot be interpreted without taking the values of the other effects into consideration.

In fact, the interaction term defined in Equation 1.4 is closely related to the odds ratio of the 2×2 table. More precisely, if the odds ratio is denoted by α, then

$$\lambda_{11}^{LP} = \frac{1}{4} log(\alpha) \qquad [1.6]$$

The logarithm of the odds ratio is equal to 0 if and only if the odds ratio is equal to 1. Therefore, independence of the two variables is equivalent to the interaction term being equal to 0. The more the values belonging to the different categories differ from 0, the stronger the corresponding effect. For the data in Table 1.2, as demonstrated by the decomposition in Table 1.14, the effect of Location on the frequencies is stronger than the effect of Preference, and the association effect is still stronger than these. (The larger the absolute value of the log-linear parameter is, the more the related multiplier in Table 1.14 differs from 1.) This interpretation does not take into account the fact that the aim of the analysis may be to analyze the effect of Location on Preference. In this case, the conditional odds of preference for a camp in the North as opposed to a camp in the South are of interest. The conditional odds when the present location is in the North, from Table 1.14, are

$$\frac{f_{11}}{f_{12}} = \frac{1,719.863 * 0.631 * 1.172 * 1.438}{1,719.863 * 0.631 * 0.853 * 0.696} \qquad [1.7]$$

$$= \frac{1.172}{0.853} * \frac{1.438}{0.696}$$

$$= 1.374 * 2.067$$

$$= 2.840$$

The general effect and the row effect cancel out from the ratio because they are the same in the numerator and the denominator. The log-linear representation leads to a multiplicative representation of the conditional odds. This representation contains two terms: One is the ratio of the multiplicative parameters related to the effect of Preference, $exp(\lambda_1^P)/exp(\lambda_2^P)$, and the other is the ratio of the two values of the multiplicative form of the interaction term, $exp(\lambda_{11}^{LP})/exp(\lambda_{12}^{LP})$. If similar conditional odds for the other category of Location are computed, one obtains that

$$\frac{f_{21}}{f_{22}} = 1.374 * 0.484 = 0.665 \qquad [1.8]$$

Here, the first multiplier is the same as before and the second one is different. The value of the first multiplier, 1.374, is the general odds for preferring a camp in the North as opposed to one in the South—this value does not depend on Location. The second multiplier is the effect of Location on the odds. The overall odds here (1.374) are very different from the *marginal odds* (1.017) that one could compute from Table 1.1. The values of the conditional odds are, however, the same as the conditional odds that could be computed from Table 1.2 (2.840 and 0.665).

In the log-linear representation outlined above, the λ, λ^P, λ^L, and λ^{PL} parameters are positive for one category and negative, with the same absolute value, for the other category (see Equation 1.3). Therefore, the parameters are balanced in the sense that they represent deviations from a certain kind of average. The related reference distribution is uniform: the "no information" or "no effect" situation is one in which the categories are equally likely. These λ parameters are used in log-linear analysis programs in BMDP (Dixon, 1981) and SPSS (Norusis, 1994).

Another approach used to define the "no information" situation is when all the observations belong to the first category (of both variables) and "effect" is deviation from this situation. In this case, the log-linear parameters are denoted by μ. The μ parameters express how much the other categories differ from the first category, or how much a joint category (i.e., a cell of the table) differs from a combination of the first categories of the variables, or cell (1, 1). Here, the first categories of the variables are used as reference categories. These are the log-linear parameters given, for example, by the GLIM program (Payne, 1986). The parameterization based on this approach is also available in certain versions of SPSS. A μ parameter is 0 if any of its indices are equal to 1. The λ and μ parameters for a 2×2 table are compared in Table 1.15.

TABLE 1.15
Log-Linear Representation With λ and μ Parameters

$\lambda + \lambda_1^R + \lambda_1^C + \lambda_{11}^{RC}$	$\lambda + \lambda_1^R + \lambda_2^C + \lambda_{12}^{RC}$
$\lambda + \lambda_2^R + \lambda_1^C + \lambda_{21}^{RC}$	$\lambda + \lambda_2^R + \lambda_2^C + \lambda_{22}^{RC}$

μ	$\mu + \mu_2^C$
$\mu + \mu_2^R$	$\mu + \mu_2^R + \mu_2^C + \mu_{22}^{RC}$

In Table 1.15, R denotes the row variable and C denotes the column variable. The application of the μ parameters is advisable when one of the categories is a *reference* category and the other categories are compared to it. The λ parameters can be used when no category is a starting point, or null value, to which the others are compared. This distinction will be more useful when tables with variables having more than two categories will be considered. The λ and μ parameters can, of course, be converted into each other (see Leimer & Rudas, 1989).

2. THE ODDS RATIOS IN $I \times J$ TABLES

Most of the important ideas and concepts in this book were introduced in the first chapter and extend easily, in many cases word for word, to general contingency tables. The generalization of the odds ratio, however, is not so straightforward. In the present chapter, the details of two kinds of generalization will be worked out to two-dimensional tables. Section A considers local odds ratios, and Section B describes the spanning cell approach to defining odds ratios for two-way tables. Both of these generalizations preserve the variation independence from the marginals. This is illustrated in Section C. Sections D, E, and F will describe some of the most important statistical models for the analysis of two-way contingency tables, such as log-linear, association, and prescribed interaction models.

A. Local Odds Ratios

One possible extension of the concept of odds ratio to general two-way tables is to consider the table with I rows and J columns as a collection of

TABLE 2.1

Local Odds Ratios for a 3×4 Table

$\dfrac{f_{11}f_{22}}{f_{12}f_{21}}$	$\dfrac{f_{12}f_{23}}{f_{13}f_{22}}$	$\dfrac{f_{13}f_{24}}{f_{14}f_{23}}$
$\dfrac{f_{21}f_{32}}{f_{22}f_{31}}$	$\dfrac{f_{22}f_{33}}{f_{23}f_{32}}$	$\dfrac{f_{23}f_{34}}{f_{24}f_{33}}$

TABLE 2.2

Preferred Camp Location of World War II American Soldiers
Cross-Classified by Location of the Present Camp

Location	Prefer to Stay	Prefer to Move			Undecided
		North	South	Undecided	
North	878	951	644	385	359
South	1,834	2,222	1,508	870	638

SOURCE: Stouffer et al. (1949).

$(I-1)(J-1)$ 2×2 tables. Each of these 2×2 tables is defined as the intersection of two adjacent rows and two adjacent columns. For every 2×2 table, the odds ratio can be computed, and the collection of these *local odds ratios* can be used to describe the association structure of the $I \times J$ table. For example, in a 2×3 table, there are two local odds ratios, one defined by the two rows (as there are no other rows) and the first two columns and the other one by the two rows and the last two columns. In a 3×3 table, there are four local odds ratios: two defined by the first and second rows, as above, and two defined by the second and third rows. The structure of local odds ratios for a 3×4 table is shown in Table 2.1.

To illustrate the computation and interpretation of the local odd ratios, a more complete form of the data presented in Table 1.2 is given in Table 2.2. The variable Preference has five categories: a preference to stay in the present camp, a preference to move to a camp in the North, a preference to move to a camp in the South, an indecision as to the location of the new camp, and an indecision whether to move or to stay. There is a slight inconsistency between the sets of data given in Tables 1.2 through 1.4 and the set of data in Table 2.2. Tables 1.2 through 1.4 were calculated using the condensed form of the data presented in Bishop and colleagues (1975) as Table 4.4-2. The data in Table 2.2 are in the form used in Goodman (1972) and by Bishop and colleagues (1975) as Table 4.4-1. The

TABLE 2.3
Local Odds Ratios of the Data in Table 2.2

1.12	1.00	0.97	0.79

sample size is 8,037 in Table 2.2, whereas the sample size is 8,036 in Tables 1.2 through 1.4, because the frequencies 1,834 and 1,508 in the second row of Table 2.2 add up to 3,342, as opposed to 3,341 in Table 2.2. This inconsistency is due to rounding.

Table 2.2 is 2×5, and there are four local odds ratios. The values of these are given in Table 2.3.

The first odds ratio is defined by the intersection of the two rows and the first and second columns. Its value is $(878 * 2,222)/(1,834 * 951) = 1.12$. The second local odds ratio is defined by the intersection of the two rows and the second and third columns. Its value is $(951 * 1,508)/(2,222 * 644) = 1.00$. The local odds ratios measure the strength of association in a small 2×2 sub-table locally, as the odds ratio does in a 2×2 table. For example, the first local odds ratio indicates that when those investigated wish either to stay in their present camps or to move to a camp in the North, then soldiers presently in the North prefer to stay in their present camps as opposed to moving to a(nother) camp in the North somewhat more strongly than soldiers presently in camps in the South. For soldiers who want to move to a specified camp in the North or South, location of the present camp does not seem to have an influence on the choice of desired location: The odds of preferring a camp in the North, as opposed to a camp in the South, are almost the same for soldiers in the North as for soldiers in the South. The other two local odds ratios can be given similar interpretations.

The local odds ratios also can be used to describe effects, or relationships, that are not local in the sense that they pertain to adjacent rows and adjacent columns. For example, if one is interested in a comparison of the odds of preferring to stay in the present camp as opposed to being undecided whether or not to move, for soldiers presently in the North and in the South, the relevant odds ratio is $(f_{11} f_{25})/(f_{21} f_{15}) = (878 * 638)/(1,834 * 359) = 0.85$. This quantity is (except for rounding error) equal to the product of all four local odds ratios. If the odds of preferring to move to an undecided location, as opposed to preferring to stay, are compared for soldiers in the North and for soldiers in the South, the relevant odds ratio is $(878 * 870)/(1,834 * 385) = 1.08$. This quantity is equal (except for rounding error) to the product of the first three odds ratios.

Let $i < i'$ be two different (but not necessarily adjacent) rows of the contingency table and $j < j'$ two different (but not necessarily adjacent) columns of the table. Then it is possible to determine the value of the odds ratio

$$\frac{f_{ij}f_{i'j'}}{f_{ij'}f_{i'j}} \tag{2.1}$$

as a function of the local odds ratios. If using the following notation for the local odds ratios of

$$\alpha_{kl} = \frac{f_{kl}f_{k+1\ l+1}}{f_{kl+1}f_{k+1l}} \tag{2.2}$$

then

$$\frac{f_{ij}f_{i'j'}}{f_{ij'}f_{i'j}} = \Pi_{i \le k < i', j \le l < j'}\alpha_{kl} \tag{2.3}$$

Together with the marginal distributions, the local odds ratios can be used to parameterize the distribution. The properties of this parameterization will be studied in Section C.

The local odds ratios compare odds of adjacent columns in adjacent rows, or the odds of adjacent rows in adjacent columns. *All* the local odds ratios jointly contain all the relevant information regarding the association structure. Whether they contain relevant information *individually* depends on whether the orderings of the categories of the variables forming the table are meaningful. This is certainly the case when the variables involved are ordinal, as in social mobility tables. There are situations, however, when a different approach to describing the association structure is more useful.

B. The Spanning Cell Approach

In the two rows of Table 2.2, it is interesting to compare the odds of preference for staying versus any other category. In this case, "preferring to stay" serves as a *reference* category to which all other categories of the variable Preference can be compared. The question asked, for instance, is this: How do the odds of preferring to stay in the present camp versus preferring to move to a camp in the South compare for soldiers in the North and in the South? To answer this question, the odds ratio is computed from four frequencies: in the two cells of the first column and in the two cells of the third column. The value of this odds ratio is $(878 * 1,508)/(1,834 * 644) = 1.12$, showing that soldiers presently in the North have a slightly

TABLE 2.4
Spanning Cell Odds Ratios for a 3×4 Table

$\dfrac{f_{11}f_{22}}{f_{12}f_{21}}$	$\dfrac{f_{11}f_{23}}{f_{13}f_{21}}$	$\dfrac{f_{11}f_{24}}{f_{14}f_{21}}$
$\dfrac{f_{11}f_{32}}{f_{12}f_{31}}$	$\dfrac{f_{11}f_{33}}{f_{13}f_{31}}$	$\dfrac{f_{11}f_{34}}{f_{14}f_{31}}$

higher chance than soldiers presently in the South to prefer staying in their present camp, as opposed to preferring to move to a camp in the South. Note, however, that both soldiers presently in the North and those presently in the South prefer to stay in their present camps over moving to a camp in the South.

When the odds of any other category of Preference are compared to the "preference to stay" category, this category serves as a reference category. Both variables in the table may have reference categories. For simplicity, it is assumed that the reference categories for both variables are their first categories. For example, when both of the variables are ordinal, the lowest categories may be selected as references. Then, the cell with two reference categories, say (1, 1), is the *reference cell.* The reference cell and any other cell that is neither in the first row nor in the first column of the table span a 2×2 sub-table. If the other cell, the *spanning cell,* is cell (i, j), with $i > 1, j > 1$, then the four cells are $(1, 1), (1, j), (i, 1), (i, j)$. In this approach to defining odds ratios for an $I \times J$ table, there is one odds ratio for every spanning cell. Every cell that is neither in the first row nor in the first column can be a spanning cell and therefore, there are $(I - 1)(J - 1)$ odds ratios. The spanning cell odds ratios for a 3×4 table, with reference cell (1, 1), are given in Table 2.4.

The spanning cell odds ratios *jointly* describe the association structure in the $I \times J$ table just like the local odds ratios do. Depending on the actual variables analyzed, the individual local or spanning cell odds ratios may be more meaningful.

When all the spanning cell odds ratios of the table are known, all other odds ratios can be computed. Let α^{kl} denote the odds ratio spanned by cell (k, l) with $k > 1, l > 1$; that is

$$\alpha^{kl} = \frac{f_{11}f_{kl}}{f_{k1}f_{1l}} \qquad [2.4]$$

Then

$$\frac{f_{ij}f_{i'j'}}{f_{ij'}f_{i'j}} = \frac{\alpha^{ij}\alpha^{i'j'}}{\alpha^{ij'}\alpha^{i'j}} \qquad [2.5]$$

for $1 < i < i'$ and $1 < j < j'$. When $i = j = 1$, the odds ratio on the left-hand side of Equation 2.5 is the spanning cell odds ratio $\alpha^{i'j'}$. When $i = 1$ but $j > 1$,

$$\frac{f_{1j}f_{i'j'}}{f_{1j'}f_{i'j}} = \frac{\alpha^{i'j'}}{\alpha^{i'j}} \qquad [2.6]$$

A similar formula applies in the $i > 1$, $j = 1$ case.

Equations 2.3 and 2.5 also can be used to convert the set of local odds ratios into the set of spanning cell odds ratios and to convert the set of spanning cell odds ratios into the set of local odds ratios. Either set of odds ratios describes the association structure in the two-way table; they contain the same information and, depending on the variables forming the table, the one with the more meaningful interpretation can be used. Both sets of odds ratios can be used, together with the marginal distributions, to parameterize the distribution in the contingency table. This parameterization is advantageous, just like in the case of 2×2 tables, because the set of odds ratios and the marginal distributions are variation independent.

There are several statistical models that are defined by restrictions on the set of odds ratios, including log-linear and various association models for the two-way table. Some of these models will be discussed in the last three sections of this chapter. The variation independence of the marginals and the set of odds ratios not only makes the odds ratios the proper parameters of association but also results in desirable properties of these statistical models. In the next section, details of the variation independence property will be considered.

C. The Variation Independence Persists

In the case of 2×2 tables, it was argued that association between the two variables forming the table could be identified with the part of the information in their joint distribution that is not contained in the marginal distributions. Therefore, association can be measured only by a parameter that is variation independent from the marginals. The odds ratio in the case of a 2×2 table is variation independent from the marginals and thus depends on the association only. Furthermore, when the marginal distributions and the odds ratio are given, the distribution is determined completely

26

TABLE 2.5
Table Containing the Desired Marginals (T)

13	23	15	19
22	47	11	20
15	20	14	31

TABLE 2.6
Table Containing the Desired Odds Ratios (U)

5	20	15	30
20	10	20	20
30	10	30	10

and, therefore, the association depends on the odds ratio only. Consequently, the odds ratio can be identified with the association.

The above argument applies word for word to $I \times J$ tables. The definition of variation independence is as follows. Let T and U be two arbitrary $I \times J$ tables. Then there exists a third $I \times J$ table V that has the same marginal distributions as T and the same odds ratios (local or spanning cell) as U. Table V with the given marginals and odds ratios can be constructed using the iterative proportional fitting procedure.

As an illustration, let the tables T and U be the ones in Table 2.5 and Table 2.6, respectively. T and U need not have the same sample size. The constructed table V will have the same number of observations as T.

The iterative proportional fitting procedure (IPFP) starts with the data in Table 2.6, the first step being row adjustment. The frequencies in the first row are multiplied by the ratio of the first row marginal frequency of T (70) to the first row marginal frequency of U (70), that is, by 1. Similarly, the second row is multiplied by $100/70 = 1.43$ and the third row by $80/80 = 1$. The table obtained after this step is performed is given in Table 2.7. The odds ratios do not change after the first step of the iterative proportional fitting. For example, the odds ratio in the upper left-hand corner of Table 2.6 is $(5 * 10)/(20 * 20) = 0.125$, which is both a local and a spanning cell odds ratio. The value of the same odds ratio in Table 2.7 is $(5 * 14.29)/(20 * 28.57) = 0.125$. (Note that the entries given in Table 2.7 are subject to rounding error.) The second step of the iterative proportional fitting procedure is a column adjustment. Here the frequencies in the first

TABLE 2.7
The Data After the First Step of IPFP

5	20	15	30
28.57	14.29	28.57	28.57
30	10	30	10

TABLE 2.8
The Data After the Second Step of IPFP

3.93	40.64	8.16	30.63
22.47	29.04	15.53	29.17
23.60	20.32	16.31	10.21

column are multiplied by $50/63.57 = 0.787$; the frequencies in the second column by $90/44.29 = 2.032$; the frequencies in the third column by $40/73.57 = 0.544$; and the frequencies in the fourth column by $70/68.57 = 1.021$. The resulting table is given in Table 2.8.

The odds ratio in the upper left-hand sub-table is $(3.93 * 29.04)/(40.64 * 22.47) = 0.125$. The odds ratios do not change in the subsequent steps of the iterative proportional fitting procedure either. The procedure converges to a table that has the same marginals as T and the same odds ratios as U.

The two variables forming the $I \times J$ table are stochastically independent if, and only if, all the odds ratios in the table are equal to 1. Equations 2.3 and 2.5 show that when all local odds ratios or all spanning cell odds ratios are equal to 1, then all other odds ratios are also equal to 1. To see that this is really equivalent to independence, let us note that independence is equivalent to every cell probability being equal to the product of the relevant row and column marginal probabilities, or $p_{ij} = p_i + p_{+j}$. When this is plugged in to any odds ratio, all terms cancel out and the value of the odds ratio is 1. On the other hand, when all the odds ratios are equal to 1, the rows of the table are proportional, implying independence.

When the local odds ratios and the marginal probabilities (or frequencies) are used to parameterize the distribution in the table, there are $(I-1)(J-1)$ local or spanning cell odds ratios, along with $I-1$ row marginals (one of the marginals is implied by the restriction on their sum), and $J-1$ column marginals. That is, $(I-1)(J-1) + I - 1 + J - 1 = IJ - 1$ parameters, which is equal to the number of cells minus one. Therefore, no parameter is redundant here, and the odds ratios plus the marginals give a one-to-one parameterization of the distribution in the table. If two distributions are different in at least one cell, then some of the odds ratios or marginals will be different. If two collections of marginals and odds ratios are different in at least one parameter, then the resulting distributions will be different. When the distribution is given, the computation of the odds ratios and marginals is straightforward, and when the odds ratios (local or spanning cell) and the marginals are given, the iterative proportional fitting procedure can be used to find the distribution.

D. Log-Linear Models and Odds Ratios

The log-linear representation of an $I \times J$ contingency table is very similar to the log-linear representation of a 2×2 table. In fact, the argument for using a log-linear representation and the definition of log-linear parameters apply word for word. The structure of log-linear representation for a 3×4 table is given in Table 2.9.

There is a log-linear parameter for the row variable, one for the column variable, and one for the association of the two variables. The parameter λ^R has I values, and the parameter μ^R has $I - 1$ values. The I values of λ^R add up to 0, but there is no similar restriction on the $I - 1$ values of μ^R. The parameter λ^C has J values that add up to 0, and the parameter μ^C has $J - 1$ values. The interaction parameter λ^{RC} has IJ values; the I values belonging to the same row or the J values belonging to the same column add up to 0. The interaction parameter μ^{RC} has $(I - 1)(J - 1)$ values. The number of *linearly independent* λ and μ parameters is the same. The meaning of this is that, for instance, when $I - 1$ out of the $I \lambda^R$ parameters are known, the last parameter can be computed without referring directly to the distribution.

Certain important properties of the distribution in an $I \times J$ table can be described well by the log-linear parameters. These properties are summarized below. Saying that a parameter is 0 is a short way of expressing that all the values of that parameter are 0.

1. The two variables forming the table are independent if, and only if, the association parameter is 0.
2. The row marginal is uniform and the row and column variables are independent if, and only if, the association parameter and the row parameter are 0.

TABLE 2.9

Log-Linear Representation of a 3×4 Table

a. λ parameters

$\lambda + \lambda_1^R +$ $\lambda_1^C + \lambda_{11}^{RC}$	$\lambda + \lambda_1^R +$ $\lambda_2^C + \lambda_{12}^{RC}$	$\lambda + \lambda_1^R +$ $\lambda_3^C + \lambda_{13}^{RC}$	$\lambda + \lambda_1^R +$ $\lambda_4^C + \lambda_{14}^{RC}$
$\lambda + \lambda_2^R +$ $\lambda_1^C + \lambda_{21}^{RC}$	$\lambda + \lambda_2^R +$ $\lambda_2^C + \lambda_{22}^{RC}$	$\lambda + \lambda_2^R +$ $\lambda_3^C + \lambda_{23}^{RC}$	$\lambda + \lambda_2^R +$ $\lambda_4^C + \lambda_{24}^{RC}$
$\lambda + \lambda_3^R +$ $\lambda_1^C + \lambda_{31}^{RC}$	$\lambda + \lambda_3^R +$ $\lambda_2^C + \lambda_{32}^{RC}$	$\lambda + \lambda_3^R +$ $\lambda_3^C + \lambda_{33}^{RC}$	$\lambda + \lambda_3^R +$ $\lambda_4^C + \lambda_{34}^{RC}$

b. μ parameters

μ	$\mu + \mu_2^C$	$\mu + \mu_3^C$	$\mu + \mu_4^C$
$\mu + \mu_2^R$	$\mu + \mu_2^R +$ $\mu_2^C + \mu_{22}^{RC}$	$\mu + \mu_2^R +$ $\mu_3^C + \mu_{23}^{RC}$	$\mu + \mu_2^R +$ $\mu_4^C + \mu_{24}^{RC}$
$\mu + \mu_3^R$	$\mu + \mu_3^R +$ $\mu_2^C + \mu_{32}^{RC}$	$\mu + \mu_3^R +$ $\mu_3^C + \mu_{33}^{RC}$	$\mu + \mu_3^R +$ $\mu_4^C + \mu_{34}^{RC}$

3. The column marginal is uniform and the row and column variables are independent if, and only if, the association parameter and the column parameter are 0.

4. The joint distribution is uniform if, and only if, all the parameters, except for λ or μ, are equal to 0.

Based on the above rules, which apply to both λ and μ parameters, the association parameter is often called the "interaction term," and the row and column parameters are often called "row and column effects." One should be careful not to think that the row parameter (or the column parameter) being equal to 0 is equivalent to the row (or column) distribution being uniform. For example, the distribution in Table 2.10 is such that

TABLE 2.10
Table With Uniform Row
Marginal and Nonzero Row Effect

10	2
5	7

the row marginal is uniform ($f_{1+} = f_{2+} = 12$), but the row effect is not 0. This is true because the average of the log-frequencies in the first row is different from the average of the log-frequencies in the second row; therefore, both of these averages are different from the average of all four log-frequencies. If independence also holds, then the two rows are proportional and, because the two marginals are the same, the rows are identical and the row effects are zero.

Just like in the 2×2 case, the log-linear interaction terms are closely related to the odds ratios. In fact, the values of the interaction term depend only on the values of the odds ratios in the table. The precise meaning of this is that if for two tables the odds ratios (local or spanning cell) are equal, then in their log-linear representations, the interaction terms (λ or μ) also are equal. Conversely, if for two tables the interaction terms in the log-linear representations are equal, then the odds ratios also are equal. This, however, does not imply that the row and column effects depend on the marginal distributions only, but the interaction terms and the other log-linear parameters are variation independent. The λ parameters are more natural to use when adjacent categories of both variables express gradual increase, and the μ parameters are more natural to use when there is a reference cell to which the others should be compared.

The more the individual values of a parameter deviate from 0, the stronger the effect expressed by the parameter. "Effect" should be understood with reference to the above rules: The row effect, for example, is a net effect after interaction is removed, which is a consequence of the variation independence of the row parameter and the interaction term. Sometimes one of the values of a parameter is much larger than all the other values. This refers to an important effect in the relevant category or cell. The λ and μ parameters should be interpreted somewhat differently: The λ values measure deviation from an average, and the μ parameters deviation from the reference cell or reference category.

The log-linear parameters of the World War II American Soldiers data presented in Table 2.2 are given in Table 2.11. The most interesting finding

TABLE 2.11
Log-linear Parameters of the
World War II American Soldiers Data

a. λ Parameters
aa. Row Effect

-0.38	0.38

ab. Column Effect

0.38	0.51	0.12	-0.41	-0.60

ac. Interaction Effect

0.01	-0.04	-0.04	-0.02	0.09
-0.01	0.04	0.04	0.02	-0.09

b. μ Parameters
ba. Row Effect

0.74

bb. Column Effect

0.08	-0.31	-0.82	-0.89

bc. Interaction Efect

0.11	0.11	0.07	-0.16

is that interaction appears to be the strongest in the undecided categories. According to what the λ parameters show, there are more soldiers presently in the North and less in the South who are undecided than there would be if there was no association among the variables. In fact, as can be computed easily from the data in Table 2.2, if Location and Preference were independent, one would expect 312 observations in cell (1,5) (as opposed to the observed 359) and 685 observations in cell (2,5) (as opposed to the observed 638).

The μ parameters show that the odds of being presently in the South, as opposed to being in the North, for those in the undecided column are less than for the other columns. This identifies the same major source of interaction as the relevant λ parameter.

Up to this point, the log-linear representation was used as a descriptive tool, providing a parameterization with desirable properties. From now on, the log-linear representation will be used as a modeling tool. Statistical models will be defined by restrictions on the log-linear parameters. These are log-linear models. We will not consider all the theoretically possible restrictions on the log-linear parameters because some of these lead to models that are difficult to estimate and interpret. Only models related to rules 1 to 4 above will be considered. These are—for reasons to be explained in Section C—called hierarchical log-linear models. The focus of interest here is interpretation and extensions of these models rather than details of model fitting. Regarding these issues, except for a few comments, the reader is referred to Bishop and colleagues (1975), Knoke and Burke (1980), and Agresti (1990).

There are four straightforward log-linear models for an $I \times J$ table:

The association parameter is 0. These are distributions for which rule 1 applies, which means that this model is equivalent to independence of the two variables.

The association and row effect parameters are 0. Here, rule 2 applies, which means that this model assumes that the row marginal distribution is uniform and the two variables are independent.

The association and the column effect parameters are 0. Here, rule 3 applies, which means that this model assumes that the column variable is uniform and the two variables are independent.

The association, the row effect, and the column effect parameters are 0. Only the constant term is present in this model. Here, rule 4 applies, which means that this model contains only the uniform distribution on the contingency table.

All these models are defined by assuming that certain log-linear parameters are equal to 0, that is, that they are not present in the log-linear representation. This assumption applied to the λ or μ log-linear parameters leads to the same model. If for a distribution some of the λ parameters are 0, then the same μ parameters are also 0 and the converse is also true. The usual way to define log-linear models is to list the parameters that are allowed to be present in the log-linear representation, that is, to list the parameters not set equal to 0. The approach here is to list those that are set to 0, which leads more directly to generalizations.

The usual procedure used to test any of the above models is to compute the maximum likelihood estimate (Eliason, 1993) of the true distribution using the observed data under the model of interest and then to compare the observed and estimated frequencies. When the observed distribution belongs to the most unlikely 1%, 5%, or 10% of the samples, then the null hypothesis, that the model under which the estimates were computed is true, is rejected.

The models considered here determine the values of some of the odds and/or odds ratios. The independence model determines that the odds ratios (local or spanning cell) are equal to 1. When there are no row and interaction effects, the odds ratios are equal to 1 and the odds comparing any two of the row marginal categories are equal to 1. Similarly, when there are no column and interaction effects, the odds ratios and the odds for the categories of the column variable are equal to 1. When only the constant term is present, the odds ratios and the odds for the categories of both variables are equal to 1. When the model is that of independence, the odds ratios are set equal to 1 by the model and the remaining parameters that must be specified for the maximum likelihood estimates are the two marginal distributions, which are taken from the observed distribution. In other words, under independence, the maximum likelihood estimate combines the prescribed odds ratios (all equal to 1) with the marginal distributions of the observed distribution. When one of the variables has odds specified by the model, then the marginal distribution of the other variable is taken from the observed distribution.

The description given above is certainly not the shortest possible characterization of the maximum likelihood estimates under log-linear models, but it admits direct generalizations to be dealt with later in this book. The construction method for the maximum likelihood estimate is the iterative proportional fitting procedure.

E. Association Models With Patterns of the Local Odds Ratios

As shown above, even the least restrictive log-linear model for an $I \times J$ table (independence) assumes that out of the $IJ - 1$ parameters, $(I - 1)$ $(J - 1)$—the values of the interaction term—are equal to 0. When this model is not an appropriate description of the population (or data) of interest, one is left with no simplified description of the data. Therefore, models that are less restrictive than the model of independence can be useful. An important class of such models is based on various assumptions regarding the pattern of local odds ratios.

The model of independence also can be formulated as a model prescribing a special pattern of local odds ratios, with all local odds ratios equal

TABLE 2.12
A 3 × 4 Table With
Uniform Local Odds Ratios

a. Frequencies

20	40	20	10
20	120	180	270
10	180	810	3,645

b. Local Odds Ratios

3	3	3
3	3	3

c. Spanning Cell Odds Ratios

3	9	27
9	81	729

to 1. The other models in this class do not assume that all the local odds ratios are equal to 1 but also do not assume that the local odds ratios are completely unstructured. The intermediate models considered here include, for example, the assumption that all the local odds ratios are equal (but not necessarily to 1) or that the local odds ratios are the same within every row.

The first and simplest (and most restrictive) of these association models assumes that the local odds ratios are equal to a common value (but this does not have to be equal to 1 as with the model of independence). This model is called *uniform association*. It allows for the existence of association among the variables forming the table, but this association, as measured by the odds ratio, is assumed to be constant locally, that is, in every 2 × 2 subtable formed by the intersection of two adjacent rows and two adjacent columns. Note that this model does not mean that there is no association or that it is weak. The association under this model may be quite strong, but it needs to be uniform. The structure of a 3 × 4 table with uniform association is illustrated in Table 2.12. In this set of data, every local odds ratio is equal to 3.

A further association model is obtained by assuming that the local odds ratios in the $I \times J$ table are constant within every row (but may be different

TABLE 2.13
A 3 × 4 Table With Row Effects
on the Local Odds Ratios

a. Frequencies

20	40	20	10
20	120	180	270
10	120	360	1,080

b. Local Odds Ratios

| 3 | 3 | 3 |
| 2 | 2 | 2 |

c. Spanning Cell Odds Ratios

| 3 | 9 | 27 |
| 6 | 36 | 216 |

across rows). This model is called the *row association* model, for it allows for row effects in the local odds ratios. Table 2.13 illustrates row effects in the local odds ratios in a 3 × 4 table.

A similar model can be defined by assuming a *column effect* in the local odds ratios. A further step in model building is to assume that there are both row and column effects present in the pattern of the local odds ratios. One way to allow for both row and column effects is to assume that every local odds ratio is a product of two effects, one constant across rows (the row effect) and the other constant across columns (the column effect). In this model, the local odds ratio α_{ij} is assumed to have the form $\alpha_{ij} = \gamma_i \delta_j$, where $\gamma_i, i = 1, \ldots, I - 1$ are the row effects and $\delta_j, j = 1, \ldots, J - 1$ are the column effects. This model is called the *row and column association* model and is usually denoted by $R+C$ because the logarithm of the local odds ratio $log(\alpha_{ij})$ is the sum of the log row effect $log(\gamma_i)$ and of the log column effect $log(\delta_j)$. Table 2.14 shows a 3 × 4 table where the $R + C$ model holds, with row effects 2 and 3 and column effects 2, 1, and 4. Note that because there are $(I - 1)(J - 1)$ local odds ratios, there are $I - 1$ row effects and $J - 1$ column effects for the local odds ratios.

The last of the commonly used association models for $I \times J$ tables assumes that logarithms of local odds ratios, rather than the local odds

TABLE 2.14
A 3 × 4 Table With Row and Column
Effects on the Local Odds Ratios

a. Frequencies

20	40	20	10
20	160	160	640
10	480	1,440	69,120

b. Local Odds Ratios

4	2	8
6	3	12

c. Spanning Cell Odds Ratios

4	8	64
24	144	13,824

ratios themselves, are products of row and column effects; that is, $log(\alpha_{ij}) = \gamma_i \delta_j$. This model is called the *row by column association* model and is usually denoted by RC. When the same row and column effects are assumed now in an RC model as above in the R+C model, the data in Table 2.15 are obtained. Note that the figures in Table 2.15 are only approximations showing the magnitude of the relevant entries. A comparison of the data in Table 2.14 and Table 2.15 shows how different the structures are under an R+C and an RC model when the parameters (the row and column effects) are the same.

The uniform, row, column, and row and column association models also can be viewed as log-linear models, but on the table of local odds ratios rather than on the table of probabilities or frequencies. When the table is of the size $I \times J$, the local odds ratios can be written into an $(I-1) \times (J-1)$ table. To this table, just like to any table of frequencies, a log-linear model can be applied. This model provides a description of the structure of association, as measured by local odds ratios. The uniform association model, assuming that the table of local odds ratios is uniform, is equivalent to assuming that in a log-linear representation of the table of local odds ratios, only the constant term (λ) is present. Similarly, the row association model for the table of frequencies is a row effect log-linear model for the table of local odds ratios. A similar statement applies to the column

TABLE 2.15

A 3 × 4 Table With Row by Column
Effects on the Local Odds Ratios

a. Frequencies

20	40	20	10
20	2,183.60	8,068.40	$1.2 * 10^7$
10	$4.4 * 10^5$	$3.3 * 10^7$	$8.0 * 10^{15}$

b. Local Odds Ratios

54.59	7.39	2,974.57
403.00	20.30	162,997.98

c. Spanning Cell Odds Ratios

54.59	403.42	$1.2 * 10^6$
$2.2 * 10^4$	$3.3 * 10^6$	$1.6 * 10^{15}$

association model. The row and column association model assumes that the local odds ratios are products of a row effect and a column effect, which is equivalent to assuming that the table of odds ratios is independent. Note that the concept of independence, defined as proportionality of rows or columns, applies to any rectangular array, not just to contingency tables. Independence is equivalent to a 0 interaction term in the log-linear representation, as it is in frequency tables. In fact, the applied procedure and arguments do not depend on the actual content of the rectangular array. It may be a contingency table filled in with frequencies just as well as a table containing local odds ratios of another (larger) table. A similar interpretation is not possible for the row by column association model. This is not log-linear but log-multiplicative because the logarithm is assumed to be a product rather than a sum.

It was shown in earlier parts of this book that the local and spanning cell odds ratios describe the association structure equally well, though from different viewpoints. Both sets of odds ratios can be used to parameterize the distribution. All the odds ratios in one set are equal to 1 if, and only if, all odds ratios in the other set are equal to 1. Therefore, the model of independence can be defined identically with the two sets of odds ratios.

TABLE 2.16
A 3 × 4 Table With Uniform
Spanning Cell Odds Ratios

a. Frequencies

20	40	20	10
20	80	40	20
10	40	20	10

b. Local Odds Ratios

2	1	1
1	1	1

c. Spanning Cell Odds Ratios

2	2	2
2	2	2

When, however, the association models considered above are defined using spanning cell odds ratios instead of local odds ratios, very different models are obtained.

Tables 2.16 to 2.18 show that the spanning cell odds ratios do not exhibit the same pattern as the local odds ratios. Table 2.16 illustrates a table where spanning cell odds ratios are constant; that is, the table is characterized by uniform spanning cell odds ratios. Table 2.17 illustrates a row effect model for the spanning cell odds ratios. Under a row and column association model for the spanning cell odds ratios, one may obtain, for example, the data in Table 2.18.

As can be seen clearly from the hypothetical sets of data presented in these tables, when one set of odds ratios has a simple pattern, the other does not necessarily have a simple pattern. Based on Equations 2.3 and 2.5, it would be easy to derive the general pattern of one set of odds ratios, supposing that the other sets can be described as being uniform or showing row and/or column effects. The practical implication is that even when a set of odds ratios does not have a simple pattern (or when in a data analytic situation the relevant hypotheses have to be rejected), the other set of odds ratios may still have a simple pattern.

TABLE 2.17
A 3 × 4 Table With Row Effects
on the Spanning Cell Odds Ratios

a. Frequencies

20	40	20	10
20	120	60	30
10	100	50	25

b. Local Odds Ratios

3	1	1
5/3	1	1

c. Spanning Cell Odds Ratios

3	3	3
5	5	5

TABLE 2.18
A 3 × 4 Table With Row and Column
Effects on the Spanning Cell Odds Ratios

a. Frequencies

20	40	20	10
20	160	40	80
10	120	30	60

b. Local Odds Ratios

4	1/2	4
3/2	1	1

c. Spanning Cell Odds Ratios

4	2	8
6	3	12

F. Prescribing the Values of the Local Odds Ratios: Generalized Log-Linear Models

Log-linear models were defined by assuming that some of the log-linear parameters are equal to 0. For cases in which this assumption was too restrictive, association models were suggested; these assume a certain pattern of the odds ratios. This section will describe another class of models related to the log-linear model. These models are defined by assuming fixed (but not necessarily 0) values of the log-linear parameters. It turns out that these models are technically very similar to the log-linear model in that specifying the values of the log-linear parameters leads to models with similar structures, whether the specified values are 0 or not. The models considered here were called generalized log-linear models by Haberman (1974) because log-linear models are special cases of the models considered here. Given that specifying the log-linear parameters is equivalent to specifying the values of the odds ratios, these models may just as well be called prescribed interaction models (Rudas, 1991; Rudas & Leimer, 1992).

In the rest of this section, only the case in which the values of the interaction term are specified will be considered. The following formula can be used to convert the μ log-linear parameters into spanning cell odds ratios, (using reference cell [1, 1]), and to convert the spanning cell odds ratios into μ parameters:

$$\alpha^{kl} = \exp(\mu_{kl}^{RC}) \qquad [2.7]$$

This formula can be checked easily using the World War II American Soldiers data presented in Table 2.2. The first spanning cell odds ratio is $(878 * 2{,}222)/(1{,}834 * 951) = 1.1186$. The first value of the μ interaction term was given in Table 2.11 as 0.11 with $\exp(0.11) = 1.1186$. Similarly, the third spanning cell odds ratio is $(878 * 870)/(1{,}834 * 385) = 1.0818$ and the third μ association term is 0.07, with $\exp(0.07) = 1.0818$.

The other relevant formulas (for the conversion of spanning cell odds ratios into λ parameters and for the conversion of local odds ratios into any log-linear parameter) are more complicated and will not be presented here; see, however, the related comments in Chapter 4 Section D.

Models prescribing the values of the odds ratios—or, equivalently, the values of the log-linear parameters—are used much less frequently than the association models described in the previous section. It seems useful, therefore, to consider these models here in more detail than the association models in the previous section. Although the general principle of parsimonious description may suggest the assumption that the odds ratios have a certain simple pattern, as with association models, it is much less clear from where the researcher may take the prescribed values. To answer this question, I will first describe the structure of the maximum likelihood estimate under a model that prescribes the values of the odds ratios. The distribution, which is the maximum likelihood estimate, is characterized by the prescribed odds ratios and by the one-way marginals of the observed table. (The iterative proportional fitting procedure can be used to calculate the estimates.) The estimates combine the prescribed odds ratios with the observed marginals. The usual testing procedure will compare this distribution to the observed one.

One problem for which models prescribing the odds ratios are used frequently is called *small area estimation*. Here, an estimate of the distribution on an $I \times J$ contingency table is required for a small area (a town or county) when the same distribution can be estimated for a larger area (an entire country) from the same or another survey or from a census. Very often, the sample size in the small area is not sufficiently large to estimate the distribution reliably. In this case, one can combine the odds ratios from the larger area with the marginals in the small area. This is the small area estimation procedure. The justification for this method is twofold. First, the estimates of the marginals may be reliable with sample sizes that do not allow for a reliable estimate of the joint distribution. This is true because both I and J are much smaller than IJ. Thus, the procedure keeps the more reliable part of information from the sample (the marginal distributions) and replaces the less reliable part (the odds ratios) by estimates based on larger sample sizes, or by true population values. This can be done because of the variation independence of the marginals and the odds ratios. Second, relationships among variables very often tend to be more stable in time and space than the distributions of the variables themselves. This justifies the assumption that the odds ratios are constant over the whole large area but that the marginals are different across the small areas involved.

When the sample size is small, some of the cell frequencies, including the zeroes in empty cells, may be poor estimates of the corresponding population quantities, and a "smoothed" version of the table may be needed. There are various techniques to apply in this situation, including the ad hoc technique of adding a constant to every frequency. One possibility for smoothing the observations is to change the table using information from prior considerations or another table. (See Chapter 12 of Bishop and colleagues [1975] for a more technical discussion of the related Bayesian analysis.) When the information borrowed is the values of the odds ratios, the result is exactly the method described above. Note that fitting a model with prescribed odds ratios in some cases provides an alternative to Bayesian methods. (See also Rudas & Leimer [1992] and the discussion in Section C of Chapter 4.)

3. 2^K TABLES

In this chapter, contingency tables of arbitrary dimension will be investigated with the restriction that all variables are assumed to be binary, or dichotomous. The concept of odds ratio, which proved to be a useful tool in analyzing two-dimensional tables, will be generalized to higher dimensional tables in Section A. The more general form is the conditional odds ratio, which preserves most of the attractive properties of the odds ratio. Variation independence remains true in this case and, for high-dimensional tables, it generalizes to a very rich collection of properties leading to a mixed parameterization of the distribution described in Section B. Section C in this chapter considers log-linear and generalized log-linear models.

A. Conditional Odds Ratios

To illustrate the possibility of extending the concept of odds ratio to multidimensional tables, a three-way version of the World War II American Soldiers data is given in Table 3.1. The variables forming the table are Preference, Location, and Region. Two 2-way marginals of this table were already presented as Tables 1.2 and 1.3. Here, again, the binary version of the variable Preference is used.

One way to use odds ratios to measure association in Table 3.1 is to consider the association between Location and Preference conditioned on the categories of Region. The part of the table in which Region is North is a 2×2 table, from which the odds ratio can be computed. This is the *conditional odds ratio* of Location and Preference, conditioned on Region = North. This conditional odds ratio will be denoted $COR(L, P|R = N)$. Its value is $(1{,}342 * 760)/(1{,}750 * 198) = 2.94$. Similarly, for the other four cells in the table $COR(L, P|R = S) = (487 * 2{,}581)/(472 * 446) = 5.97$.

The conclusion is that for soldiers whose region of origin is in the South, the effect of Location on Preference is stronger than for those whose region

TABLE 3.1

Preferred Camp Location of World War II
American Soldiers Cross-Classified by Location
of the Present Camp and Region of Origin

Region	Location	Preference	
		North	South
North	North	1,342	198
	South	1,750	760
South	North	487	446
	South	472	2,581

SOURCE: Stouffer, et al. (1949).

of origin is in the North. The following ratio of the two conditional odds ratios expresses relative strength of the above effect for those whose region of origin is in the North as compared with those from the South.

$$\frac{COR(L, P|R = N)}{COR(L, P|R = S)} = 0.49 \qquad [3.1]$$

It was shown in Chapter 1 that the odds ratio between Location and Preference is 4.27. The conditional odds ratios of these two variables, conditioned on fixed categories of Region, are 2.94 and 5.97. That is, the effect of Location on Preference is different depending on whether all the soldiers, or only soldiers from the North, or only soldiers from the South are considered. Therefore, Region influences the effect of Location on Preference.

The data in Table 3.1 also make it possible to compute the *COR* of Region and Preference given Location. *COR(R, P|L = N)* = (1,342 * 446)/ (487 * 198) = 6.21, and *COR(R, P|L = S)* = (1,750 * 2,581)/(472 * 760) = 12.59. Therefore, the odds for preferring a camp in the North, as opposed to one in the South, are about six times as high for soldiers who come from the North than for soldiers who come from the South, if only soldiers presently in the North are considered. The same effect is about twice as large for soldiers presently in the South. More precisely, the following ratio of the two conditional odds ratios is obtained:

$$\frac{COR(R, P|L = N)}{COR(R, P|L = S)} = 0.49 \qquad [3.2]$$

A comparison of Equations 3.1 and 3.2 gives a somewhat surprising result in that the ratio of the two conditional odds ratios is the same whether the odds ratios conditioned on Location or those conditioned on Region are considered. When computed, the conditional odds ratios of Region and Location given Preference also would be 0.49. From this, one may conclude that the ratio of the two conditional odds ratios is a quantity that is characteristic of the three-dimensional distribution but does not depend on which variable is in the condition. The effect that any variable can have on the association between the two other variables is constant for a table. This quantity is called the *second-order odds ratio* because it measures association between three, not two, variables. The second-order odds ratio, or second-order association term, is equal to

$$\frac{f_{111} f_{122} f_{212} f_{221}}{f_{222} f_{211} f_{121} f_{112}} \qquad [3.3]$$

To illustrate the significance of the second-order association, Table 3.2 contains a set of data in which the value of the second-order association term is 1, but all two-way marginal distributions are identical to the corresponding two-way marginals in Table 3.1. The procedure that can be used to generate such a table and further properties of a table like this will be discussed in Section B.

For the hypothetical set of data in Table 3.2, $COR(L, P|R = N) = (1,388.98 * 806.98)/(1,703.02 * 151.02) = 4.36$ and $COR(L, P|R = S) = (440.02 * 2,534.02)/(518.98 * 492.98) = 4.36$. That is, the two conditional odds ratios are equal but are not equal to the unconditional, or marginal, odds, ratio, which was found to be equal to 4.27. Similarly, the two conditional odds ratios of Region and Preference are $COR(R, P|L = N) = 10.30$ and $COR(R, P|L = S) = 10.30$. The values of the conditional odds ratios do not depend on the conditioning categories because the second order odds ratio—that is, the ratio of these two values—was set at one.

The second-order association term, or second-order odds ratio, in Equation 3.3 measures the part of the association among the three variables that cannot be attributed to any two from among the variables. There is no way to find out the value of the second-order odds ratio in a three-way table if only the two-way marginals are known. In fact, as will be described in the next section, any set of two-way marginals can be combined with any second-order association, which is a generalization of the variation independence considered earlier.

For a four-dimensional table, the odds ratio can be defined fixing one category of the fourth variable. This, in turn, leads to a $2 \times 2 \times 2$ subtable

TABLE 3.2

Hypothetical Set of Data Derived From the Data in Table 3.1
by Removal of the Second Order Association

Region	Location	Preference	
		North	South
North	North	1,388.98	151.02
	South	1,703.02	806.98
South	North	440.02	492.98
	South	518.98	2,534.02

of the original table, which is a conditional table because all observations in this subtable are characterized by the fixed value, of say 1, of the fourth variable. In this $2 \times 2 \times 2$ table, the odds ratio in Equation 3.3 can be computed which is the conditional odds ratio of the first three variables, given that the fourth is equal to 1. If the variables are denoted by A, B, C, and D, then

$$COR(A, B, C|D = 1) = \frac{f_{1111} f_{1221} f_{2121} f_{2211}}{f_{2221} f_{2111} f_{1211} f_{1121}} \qquad [3.4]$$

The formula in Equation 3.4 is obtained from Equation 3.3 by adding a fourth index (equal to 1) to all cells. Similarly, $COR(A, B, C|D = 2)$ could be obtained by replacing the last index in Equation 3.4 by 2. To explore some of the properties of the conditional odds ratio defined in Equation 3.4, Table 3.3 contains a four-dimensional version of the World War II American Soldiers data. Two-way marginals of this set of data were given in Tables 1.2, 1.3, and 1.4.

The conditional odds ratio of Region, Location, and Preference, given that Race is Black, is

$$COR(R, L, P|Ra = \text{Black}) = \frac{387 * 250 * 270 * 381}{36 * 876 * 383 * 1,712} = 0.48 \qquad [3.5]$$

This is a second order odds ratio, computed for black soldiers only. The same quantity for white soldiers is

$$COR(R, L, P|Ra = \text{White}) = \frac{955 * 510 * 176 * 91}{162 * 874 * 104 * 869} = 0.61 \qquad [3.6]$$

TABLE 3.3

Preferred Camp Location of World War II
American Soldiers Cross-Classified by Location
of the Present Camp, Region of Origin, and Race

Race	Region	Location	Preference	
			North	South
Black	North	North	387	36
		South	876	250
	South	North	383	270
		South	381	1,712
White	North	North	955	162
		South	874	510
	South	North	104	176
		South	91	869

SOURCE: Stouffer et al. (1949).

Therefore, one may conclude that the association among Region, Location, and Preference is stronger for white soldiers than for black soldiers. Note that the above statement refers to the net association among the three variables after pairwise associations have been removed. The ratio of the above conditional odds ratios is $0.48/0.61 = 0.79$. The same value would be obtained if ratios of second-order odds ratios conditioned on any other variable were computed. Just as in the case of three-dimensional tables, this common ratio is characteristic of the four-way table and is called the *third-order odds ratio* of the table. This measures association among the four variables that cannot be attributed to any three from among them and has the following general form:

$$\frac{f_{1111} f_{1122} f_{1212} f_{1221} f_{2112} f_{2121} f_{2211} f_{2222}}{f_{2111} f_{1211} f_{1121} f_{1112} f_{1222} f_{2122} f_{2212} f_{2221}} \qquad [3.7]$$

The first- and second-order conditional odds ratios in a table are connected to each other, as is illustrated by the following formula:

$$\frac{COR(R, P|L = N, Ra = B)}{COR(R, P|L = S, Ra = B)} = COR(R, L, P|Ra = B) \qquad [3.8]$$

The second- and third-order odds ratios above can be generalized to any number of variables. For K variables, one has an odds ratio of order $i-1$, which is a ratio with the product of 2^{K-1} cell frequencies (or probabilities) in the numerator and the product of the remaining 2^{K-1} cell frequencies (or probabilities) in the denominator (note that $2^{K-1} + 2^{K-1} = 2^K$). The following rule can be applied to determine which cell frequencies (or probabilities) are in the numerator and which ones are in the denominator: Cells with an even number of 2 indices are in the numerator, and cells with an odd number of 2 indices are in the denominator. This is equivalent to saying that if K is even, then cells with an even number of 1 indices are in the numerator; and if K is odd, then cells with an odd number of 1 indices are in the numerator. The odds ratios of order $K - 1$ measure that part of the association among the K variables that cannot be attributed to any subset of the variables. The justification for this statement is related to a variation independence property that will be considered in the next section. Technically, an odds ratio of order $K - 1$ is the ratio of two conditional odds ratios, both computed for $K - 1$ variables, with the Kth variable fixed as a condition at its two different values. This ratio will be the same, independently of the choice of the variable in the condition.

One can condition not only on one variable but also on an arbitrary number of variables. The K variables forming the table can be divided into two parts containing, for example, L and $K - L$ variables. When the $K - L$ variables are fixed at arbitrary values, there are 2^L cells which have these values on the $K - L$ variables fixed. For example, the data in Table 3.3 is a $2 \times 2 \times 2 \times 2$ table, which means $K = 4$. If, for example, variables Race and Region are fixed at the values Black and North, respectively, then there are four cells with these indices for these variables: (1, 1, 1, 1), (1, 1, 1, 2), (1, 1, 2, 1), (1, 1, 2, 2). These cells have the fixed indices for the first two variables and, for the remaining two variables, all possible combinations are present, yielding a total of 4 ($= 2^2$) cells. In general, the 2^L cells form a contingency table. The odds ratio in this L dimensional table is the conditional odds ratio of the L variables given the fixed categories of the other $K–L$ variables. In the example, the conditional odds ratio of variables Location and Preference, given that Race is Black and Region is North, is

$$COR(L, P|Ra = \text{Black}, R = \text{North}) = \frac{f_{1111}f_{1122}}{f_{1112}f_{1121}} = \frac{387 * 250}{876 * 36} = 3.07 \quad [3.9]$$

The structure of the above conditional odds ratio is such that, disregarding the first two indices with fixed values, it is an odds ratio for the other two variables. The conditional odds ratio in Equation 3.9 measures association between the variables Location and Preference for black soldiers whose region of origin is the North. Generally, there are 2^{K-L} conditional odds

48

TABLE 3.4

Conditional Odds Ratios Between Location and Preference
Given Race and Region for the Data in Table 3.3

	Region	
Race	North	South
Black	3.07	6.37
White	3.44	5.64

SOURCE: Stouffer et al. (1949).

ratios, exactly as many as the number of cells for the $K - L$ variables in the condition. In our example, there are four conditional odds ratios of the type given in Equation 3.9. These measure association between Location and Preference in all possible combinations of Race and Region. The values of these conditional odds ratios are given in Table 3.4.

The conditional odds ratios in Table 3.4 can be given the following interpretation: The effect of Location on Preference depends very little on Race but depends heavily on Region. Almost independently of Race, this effect is about twice as large for soldiers who come from the South as for soldiers from the North. For the former group of soldiers, the odds of preferring a camp in the North (as opposed to one in the South) are about six times as great for soldiers presently in the North than for soldiers presently in the South. For the latter group of soldiers, that is, soldiers who come from the North, those who are presently in the North prefer a camp in the North over a camp in the South about three times more than those presently in the South. The only (relatively small) effect of Race is that the ratio of the conditional odds ratios is greater than 2 for black soldiers and less than 2 for white soldiers, which means the effect described above is somewhat more marked for black soldiers than for white soldiers.

It follows from the definition of the conditional odds ratio that, if in a $2 \times 2 \times 2$ table the conditional odds ratios of two variables, given both values of the third variable, are known, then the second-order odds ratio of the three variables can be computed. If in a $2 \times 2 \times 2 \times 2$ table the conditional odds ratios of any two variables, say A and B, given all four possible combinations of the other two variables, say C and D, are known, then the conditional odds ratios of A, B, and C, given both values of D, and the conditional odds ratios of A, B, and D, given both values of C, can be computed using the following formulas:

$$COR(A, B, C|D = l) = \frac{COR(A, B|C = 1, D = l)}{COR(A, B|C = 2, D = l)} \qquad [3.10]$$

$$COR(A, B, D|C = k) = \frac{COR(A, B|C = k, D = 1)}{COR(A, B|C = k, D = 2)} \qquad [3.11]$$

Furthermore, the third-order odds ratio of A, B, C, and D can also be computed as:

$$COR(A, B, C, D) = \frac{COR(A, B, C|D = 1)}{COR(A, B, C|D = 2)} = \frac{COR(A, B, D|C = 1)}{COR(A, B, D|C = 2)} \qquad [3.12]$$

The general form of this property is that if all the conditional odds ratios of a given subset of the variables are known ("all" meaning for every possible combination of the categories of the remaining variables), then the conditional odds ratios of any other subset of variables which contains the original subset, for any combination of the categories of the remaining variables, are also known.

A collection of subsets of the set of variables forming the table is an *ascending class of subsets*, if the following is true: If a subset is contained in the class, then any other subset containing the former one as a subset is also contained in the class. For example, if the table is formed by variables A, B, C, D, and E, then $\{ABC, ABCD, ABCDE\}$ is not an ascending class, because it does not contain $ABCE$ (this contains ABC, which is contained in the class). The following class is ascending: $\{ABC, ABD, ABCD, ABCE, ABDE, ABCDE\}$. Every ascending class contains smallest subsets in the sense that no subsets of these are included. In the previous ascending class, the smallest, or minimal, subsets are ABC and ABD. Every ascending class is completely determined by its minimal subsets. These minimal subsets are said to generate the ascending class of subsets. The ascending class generated by a collection of subsets is the one containing any subset of the variables that is larger than the given ones. Using the concept of ascending class, one may say that conditional odds ratios are always defined on an ascending class of subsets. If, for a subset of variables, all conditional odds ratios are given, then all conditional odds ratios for the subsets in the ascending class generated by the first subset are also given. This remains true if one starts with all the conditional odds ratios of several subsets of variables. The ascending systems defined here will play an important role in the variation independence property of the odds ratios and marginals and in the resulting mixed parameterization.

At first sight, the collection of *marginal* odds ratios may seem just as natural a generalization of the odds ratio in two-way tables as the collection

TABLE 3.5

Hypothetical Set of Data

Illustrating Simpson's Paradox

		C	
A	B	1	2
1	1	100	1,000
	2	1	200
2	1	200	1
	2	1,000	100

of *conditional* odds ratios. Marginal odds ratios, however, suffer from serious drawbacks. From Table 3.1, which is a marginal of Table 3.3, one obtains a conditional odds ratio of Location and Preference, when conditioned on Region = North, of 2.94. Table 3.4 shows that the same conditional odds ratio, when further conditioned on either black or white soldiers, gives a larger value. This means that the effect of Location on Preference for soldiers coming from the North is weaker than the same effect calculated for black soldiers or white soldiers. Even more surprising may be the set of hypothetical data given in Table 3.5.

In Table 3.5, $COR(B, C|A = 1) = 20$ and $COR(B, C|A = 2) = 20$, but the marginal odds ratio of variables B and C is $(300 * 300)/(1,001 * 1,001) = 0.09$. That is, both conditional odds ratios show a "positive" association, but the marginal odds ratio shows a "negative" association. This phenomenon is called Simpson's paradox. The morals are that the results of every analysis depend heavily on the variables involved and conditional and marginal odds ratios measure different things.

B. Mixed Parameterization of the Cell Probabilities

The main topic in this section is the variation independence between odds ratios and marginal distributions for the case of 2^K tables and the mixed parameterization of the distribution based on the variation independence property.

In the previous section, conditional odds ratios were defined on an ascending system of subsets in the sense that if all the conditional odds ratios are known for a subset of the variables, then the conditional odds ratios also are known for subsets of variables contained in the ascending system generated by the original subset. Marginal distributions of a multi-dimensional contingency table have a related property. This follows from the simple fact that if, for example, the joint marginal distribution of variables A, B, and C is known, then at the same time, the joint marginal of A and B or the marginal of C also are known.

This property is described more generally using the concept of descending systems of subsets. A class of subsets of the variables is called *descending* if, with every subset in the class, all other subsets contained within it also are in the class. For example, for variables A, B, C, D, and E, the class $\{A, B, C, AB, AC, ABC\}$ is not descending because it does not contain BC, in spite of the fact that it contains ABC, and BC is a subset of ABC. Every descending class of subsets contains maximal elements, which characterize the descending class. A subset in a class of subsets is maximal if there is no subset in the class that contains it. All subsets of these maximal elements belong to the descending class. Marginal distributions in a contingency table are always determined on a descending class of subsets, because with every marginal distribution, all lower dimensional marginals contained in it also are given.

Ascending and descending classes of subsets of variables are related to each other. The complement of an ascending class, with respect to the class of all subsets of variables, is descending, and the complement of a descending class, with respect to the class of all subsets, is ascending. To illustrate this, listed below are all the subsets of three variables:

$$ABC$$
$$AB, AC, BC$$
$$A, B, C$$
$$\varnothing$$

There is a partial ordering among the subsets. For example, B and AB can be compared, and AB is larger than B because the latter is contained in the former. Subsets B and AC cannot be compared because neither one of them contains the other. Therefore, the ordering is only partial. The above list is such that for any subset, all larger subsets are in rows above this subset and all the smaller ones are below this subset. Here $\{A, AB, AC, ABC\}$ is an ascending system, and its complement is $\{\varnothing, B, C, BC\}$, a descending system. For five variables, the partial ordering takes the following form:

$$\overline{\text{ABCDE}}$$
$$\overline{\text{ABCD}}, \overline{\text{ABCE}}, \underline{\text{ABDE}}, \overline{\text{ACDE}}, \overline{\text{BCDE}}$$
$$\underline{\text{ABC}}, \underline{\text{ABD}}, \underline{\text{ABE}}, \overline{\text{ACD}}, \underline{\text{ADE}}, \overline{\text{ACE}}, \overline{\text{BCD}}, \overline{\text{BCE}}, \underline{\text{BDE}}, \overline{\text{CDE}}$$
$$\underline{\text{AB}}, \underline{\text{AC}}, \underline{\text{AD}}, \underline{\text{AE}}, \underline{\text{BC}}, \underline{\text{BD}}, \underline{\text{BE}}, \overline{\text{CD}}, \overline{\text{CE}}, \underline{\text{DE}}$$
$$\underline{\text{A}}, \underline{\text{B}}, \underline{\text{C}}, \underline{\text{D}}, \text{E}$$
$$\varnothing$$

As an example, let us consider the descending system generated by subsets *ABC* and *ABDE*. This class contains the underlined subsets. The complement of this descending system is an ascending system with the minimal elements *CD* and *CE*.

Now we are ready to formulate the variation independence property for 2^K tables. To do this, let us consider an ascending class of subsets of the variables and the conditional odds ratios of these subsets. This means all the conditional odds ratios belonging to these subsets. For every subset in the class, the conditioning variables in the conditional odds ratios are all the variables not contained in this subset. Let us consider the conditional odds ratios for all possible joint categories of the conditioning variables. Moreover, consider the complement of the ascending system, which is a descending system, and the marginal distributions of the subsets in this descending class. Then the conditional odds ratios on the ascending system and the marginal distributions on the descending system are variation independent.

For example, it was established above that in the case of five variables, the descending system, with maximal subsets *ABC* and *ABDE,* and the ascending system, with minimal elements *CD* and *CE,* are complements. Then the conditional odds ratios of *CD,* for any fixed value of *ABE,* and the conditional odds ratios of *CE,* for any fixed value of *ABD* (and all the conditional odds ratios generated by these), are variation independent from the marginal distributions of *ABC* and *ABDE* (and the marginals generated by these).

An appropriate form of the iterative proportional fitting procedure can be used to construct the distribution with the prescribed marginals (on the descending system) and with the prescribed conditional odds ratios (on the ascending system that is the complement of the previous descending system). The procedure starts with a distribution that has the prescribed conditional odds ratios. Then, marginal adjustments are applied to make the marginals on the descending system equal to the prescribed ones without changing the conditional odds ratios on the ascending system. The marginal adjustments are applied in cycles consisting of adjustments pertaining to all maximal elements in the descending system on which the marginals are prescribed. For instance, in the above example, marginal adjustments are needed only for the subsets ABC and $ABDE$. If the marginal distributions of these subsets are as required, then the marginal distributions of any subset contained in the generated descending system are as required, as well.

The adjustment pertaining to a marginal consists of multiplying every cell frequency by the ratio of the desired marginal of that cell, according to the relevant subset of variables, to the actual marginal of that subset. In the above example, the marginal adjustment pertaining to subset ABC means that the f_{ijklm} frequency in cell (i, j, k, l, m) is multiplied by the ratio r_{ijk++}/f_{ijk++}, where r_{ijk++} is the required marginal frequency in the (i, j, k) cell of the ABC marginal, and f_{ijk++} is the frequency in the same marginal cell computed from the actual distribution. Similar adjustments are applied for every maximal subset in the descending system. The cycles of these adjustments are repeated until convergence is achieved.

The marginal distributions on the descending system and the conditional odds ratios on the ascending system (if these two systems are complements to each other) uniquely determine the distribution. There is only one distribution on the contingency table that has both the prescribed marginals and the prescribed conditional odds ratios. Obviously, the distribution also uniquely determines the marginals on the descending system and the conditional odds ratios on the ascending system; therefore, the marginals and the conditional odds ratios give a parameterization of the distribution on the contingency table. This parameterization is based on splitting the class of all subsets of the variables into two parts: a descending system and an ascending system. The parameters that describe the distribution are the marginals on the descending system and the conditional odds ratios on the ascending system. This is called a *mixed parameterization* because two kinds of parameters (marginals and conditional odds ratios) are involved. The two groups of parameters in this mixed parameterization are variation independent.

Both groups of parameters in a mixed parameterization are based on subsets of variables; however, the subsets in the two groups play very different roles. The marginal distributions show that part of the information in the table that could be obtained if only that group of variables was observed (and the others were not). This shows the relationship among these variables, disregarding the other variables, and is called the *marginal* effect of the subset of variables. On the other hand, the parameters pertaining to the subsets in the ascending system describe the relationship among these variables conditioned on the other variables. This is called the *partial* association among these variables. This is the association that can be measured only when all other variables are also taken into consideration. Many of the widely used models for contingency tables are based on the above separation of information and are reviewed in the next section.

C. Log-Linear and Generalized Log-Linear Models

It follows from Equations 3.10 and 3.11 (and their generalizations) that if all conditional odds ratios given are equal to 1, then the odds ratios of all subsets in the ascending system are equal to 1 as well. This is true because 1 divided by 1 is 1. That is, if the conditional odds ratios pertaining to the minimal elements of an ascending class of subsets are equal to 1, then all the odds ratios are equal to 1 in the ascending system. *A log-linear model is the assumption that the conditional odds ratios pertaining to an ascending class of subsets are all equal to one.*

There are several other definitions of log-linear models available. The most widely used (see, e.g., Agresti, 1990) is based on log-linear parameters and the log-linear representation. With this definition, log-linear parameters need to be defined separately for three-, four-, five-, and higher-dimensional tables, which requires attention to many technical details. There is a coordinate-free approach (see Haberman, 1974) that can be applied to this definition, but it is quite demanding mathematically. The introduction of the log-linear model based on log-linear representation usually is motivated by its similarity to the multiway analysis of variance.

An alternative approach to the definition and interpretation of log-linear models is through information theoretic considerations (see Gokhale & Kullback, 1978). It can be proved that, from among all the distributions that have certain prescribed marginal distributions, the one closest to the uniform distribution can be written in a special form, and this special form is the log-linear model. Here, the distance of two distributions is measured by a directed divergence measure that can be given an information theoretic interpretation. This approach, even though it has several theoretical advantages, is quite involved mathematically.

A third approach, which does not lead to the definition and interpretation of all log-linear models, is based on postulating a certain Markov property, that is, a collection of conditional independence statements. This approach only leads to the so-called graphical log-linear models (see Darroch, Lauritzen, & Speed, 1980, and Whittaker, 1990) but makes a very useful interpretation of these models possible.

Here, yet another definition of log-linear models based on conditional odds ratios is given. The advantages of this definition include that it is elementary, is coordinate-free, has straightforward interpretation, and leads naturally to the properties of the maximum likelihood estimates.

According to the definition provided here, the various log-linear models are obtained by different choices of the ascending class, where the conditional odds ratios are set equal to 1. The connection with the usual definition of log-linear models is established by the following result:

For a distribution on the contingency table, the conditional odds ratios pertaining to an ascending class of subsets are all equal to one if, and only if, the log-linear parameters pertaining to the subsets in the ascending class are all equal to zero.

This means that setting the conditional odds ratios on an ascending system equal to 1 is equivalent to allowing log-linear parameters to be present (i.e., to be different from 0) on the descending class of subsets, which is the complement of the ascending class. Log-linear parameters for 2^K tables are usually defined by a direct generalization of the procedure described in Capter 1 Section C.

A special case of the statement above was already seen in Chapter 1 Section C, where the relationship between the odds ratio and the log-linear interaction parameter was discussed for a 2×2 table. The interaction parameter was 0 if, and only if, the odds ratio was equal to 1. In the case of 2^K tables, a similar but more general relationship holds.

In the most common definition of log-linear models, some of the log-linear parameters are allowed to be different from 0. The selection of these parameters defines the model. The requirement that, together with a log-linear parameter, any other log-linear parameter pertaining to a subset of the variables associated with the first parameter must be present, is called the *hierarchy* principle. For example, if in a four-way table, formed by the variables A, B, C, and D, in a log-linear model a parameter pertaining to ABC is present, then the parameters pertaining to AB, AC, BC, A, B, C, and $\emptyset$ (the parameter associated with $\emptyset$ is the constant term) should also be present. Log-linear models in the remainder of this book will always be hierarchical log-linear models.

In log-linear analysis, the maximal subsets in the descending system are usually called "maximal interactions" and are used to give a simple description of the model. The term *maximal interaction* refers to a maximal subset that has a conditional odds ratio (conditioned on all other variables) different from 1.

What interpretation can be given to a log-linear model? If the conditional odds ratios of a set of variables, given all other variables, are equal to 1, for all possible combinations of the conditioning variables, then there is no conditional association among these variables that would not be present in some of the subsets of this set. In other words, subsets of this set may have associations within them, but the actual set shows no additional conditional association. A possible interpretation of lack of conditional association is that the association among these variables can be accounted for by the other variables: When the other variables are held constant, association among these variables vanishes. When these variables are analyzed marginally (that is, without conditioning on the other variables), they may show association.

The above interpretive statements are the most interesting when applied to the minimal elements in the ascending class. These subsets of variables do not have conditional association that could not be attributed to some of their subsets; however, all of their subsets are allowed to have conditional association that cannot be attributed to their subsets, because the subsets of the minimal elements are not contained in the ascending system.

Suppose, for example, that the distribution in Table 3.2 (when converted from frequencies to probabilities) describes the true distribution in the underlying population. In this table, the second-order association was removed from the original data. Therefore, in this distribution all association among Preference, Location, and Region can be attributed to one or more pairs of the variables. On the other hand, any pair of the variables is allowed to have conditional association (conditioned on the third variable) that cannot be attributed to the third variable.

Because of the *regression-type* problem considered (i.e., the goal of the analysis is to model the effects of Location and Region on Preference), there is another possible interpretation: Both explanatory variables have effects on the dependent variable, and the lack of second-order association implies that these effects can be separated, or that their joint effect can be attributed entirely to their separate effects. The lack of second-order association is equivalent to the following log-linear representation:

$$\log P_{ijk} = \lambda + \lambda_i^P + \lambda_j^L + \lambda_k^R + \lambda_{ij}^{PL} + \lambda_{ik}^{PR} + \lambda_{jk}^{LR} \qquad [3.13]$$

By exponentiating both sides and denoting $\exp(\lambda)$ with β, one obtains that

$$P_{ijk} = \beta \beta_i^P \beta_j^L \beta_k^R \beta_{ij}^{PL} \beta_{ik}^{PR} \beta_{jk}^{LR} \qquad [3.14]$$

Then,

$$\frac{P_{Njk}}{P_{Sjk}} = \frac{\beta\beta_N^P\beta_j^L\beta_k^R\beta_{Nj}^{PL}\beta_{Nk}^{PR}\beta_{jk}^{LR}}{\beta\beta_S^P\beta_j^L\beta_k^R\beta_{Sj}^{PL}\beta_{Sk}^{PR}\beta_{jk}^{LR}} \qquad [3.15]$$

where both j and k can be either North or South. After cancelling the identical terms in the numerator and denominator, one obtains that

$$\frac{P_{Njk}}{P_{Sjk}} = \frac{\beta_N^P\,\beta_{Nj}^L\,\beta_{Nk}^{PR}}{\beta_S^P\,\beta_{Sj}^L\,\beta_{Sk}^{PR}} \qquad [3.16]$$

That is, the odds of preferring a camp in the North, as opposed to a camp in the South, for category j of Location and category k of Region are a product of three terms. The first one does not depend on j and k and is the value of the general odds. The second one depends on the category of Location only and represents the effect of this variable on the conditional odds. The third term depends on the category of variable Region only and represents the effect of this variable on the conditional odds.

The effects of the explanatory variables on the odds of the dependent variable can be separated because there is no second-order association. If second-order association was present in the example, then the odds of Preference could be represented as a four-term product, where the fourth term refers to the joint effect of the explanatory variables on the odds of the dependent variable that cannot be attributed to these variables separately.

In practical data analytic situations, the test of fit of the model is usually based on a comparison of the maximum likelihood estimates, therefore, with the observed frequencies. Computation of the maximum likelihood estimates therefore plays a central role in any model-based analysis. The maximum likelihood estimate of a distribution under a log-linear model has the following mixed parameterization: On the ascending system, the conditional odds ratios are all equal to 1 (as prescribed by the model), and the marginal distributions on the complement descending system are equal to the corresponding observed marginal distributions. In other words, the maximum likelihood estimate combines the prescribed conditional odds ratios with the observed marginals.

The maximum likelihood estimates can be obtained by an appropriate version of the iterative proportional fitting procedure. For example, when the observations are the data in Table 3.1 and the model is that of no second-order association (or, equivalently, no second-order interaction), then the maximum likelihood estimates are the frequencies given in Table 3.2. The relevant test of fit leads to a chi-squared statistic of 34.85 on 1 degree of freedom, suggesting that the hypothesis is not appropriate. Therefore, the separation of the effect of Location and Region on the odds of Preference, as described above, is not possible: The two explanatory variables have a joint effect on the odds that cannot be attributed to either one of them.

The data in Table 3.3 can be described by a log-linear model with the following maximal interactions (chi-squared statistic: 1.45, degrees of freedom: 3, tail probability: 0.69): {Race, Region, Location}; {Race, Preference}; and {Region, Location, Preference}. These are the maximal elements of the descending system. The minimal elements of the ascending system are {Race, Region, Preference} and {Race, Location, Preference}. In this model, there are no conditional associations within the last two groups of variables that could not be attributed to some of their subsets. In other words, Race and Region do not have a joint effect on Preference that could not be attributed to either Race or Region. Similarly, Race and Location do not have a joint effect on Preference that could not be attributed to the effect of Race or to that of Location. According to this model, the conditional odds of the two categories of Preference, given all other variables, can be written in a product form with the following factors: general odds, separate effects of Race, Region, and Location, and joint effect of Region and Location. Region and Location have a joint effect on the odds of Preference, but the other two pairs of explanatory variables, Race and Region or Race and Location, do not have joint effects. Consequently, the three explanatory variables do not have a joint effect on Preference. A joint effect here means a "net" effect, that is, one that cannot be attributed to smaller subsets.

Generalized log-linear models (Haberman, 1974) are also best characterized as models prescribing the values of some of the conditional odds ratios; therefore, they can be called prescribed conditional interaction models (Rudas, 1991). When some of the conditional odds ratios (for all possible values of the conditioning variables) are prescribed, then, at the same time, the conditional odds ratios of any subset of the variables containing these also are prescribed (for all possible values of the conditioning variables of these sets). When the prescribed values are not all equal to 1, one obtains a generalized log-linear model. Both log-linear and generalized log-linear models are prescribed conditional interaction (or association) models. In the usual log-linear models, the conditional odds ratios are all prescribed to be equal to 1, and in generalized log-linear models, to some other values. When the values of the conditional odds ratios are prescribed, the values of the log-linear parameters are also prescribed on the same ascending system. In the case of log-linear models, the parameters pertaining to the subsets in the ascending system are set to 0, and in generalized log-linear models, to other values.

It is possible to work out the formulae that can be used to convert conditional odds ratios into log-linear parameters and vice versa (see Chapter 4 Section D). These formulae are useful when a distribution with the prescribed conditional odds ratios is sought, for instance, to start the iterative proportional fitting procedure (see below). The values of the log-linear parameters obtained can be used to construct this distribution.

These models can be given two kinds of interpretation. The values of the conditional odds ratios give the amount (as measured by the odds ratio) of conditional association present in the relevant subset in excess of the conditional association, which can be attributed to the subsets of this subset. Another interpretation is appropriate when the model is formulated in such a way that there is a fixed distribution with the given conditional odds ratios. This distribution, say R, serves as a reference distribution, and all other distributions in the model have the same conditional odds ratios on the ascending system as the reference distribution. Let P be any distribution from the model, and write into every cell in the table the ratio of the relevant probabilities from P and R. If, for example, the table is three-dimensional, write into cell $(1, 2, 1)$ the quantity P_{121}/R_{121}. This table is not a probability distribution; however, conditional odds ratios can be computed from it just like in the case of probability distributions. Then the model contains exactly those distributions P for which the conditional odds ratios, computed from the above ratio table, pertaining to the subsets in the ascending class are equal to 1. In other words, the *relative conditional odds ratios* are equal to 1.

The maximum likelihood estimates under a generalized log-linear model combine the prescribed conditional odds ratios on the ascending system with the observed marginals on the complement descending system and can be obtained by the iterative proportional fitting procedure, which may begin with R. For applications of generalized log-linear models, see the comments in Chapter 4 Section C.

4. GENERAL TABLES

In this chapter, the general concept of conditional odds ratios introduced in Chapter 3 is extended to polytomous variables. This is done in Section A by using the approaches of local and spanning cell odds ratios already considered in Chapter 2. Section B discusses variation independence of the odds ratios and of the marginal distribution and introduces the mixed parameterization of the distribution based on these parameters. Some of the most important log-linear and other association models for general contingency tables are presented in Section C as structured restrictions on some of the parameters in the mixed parameterization. Finally, Section D discusses the relationship between log-linear parameters and conditional odds ratios, providing appealing interpretations of several log-linear models.

A. Conditional Local or Spanning Cell Odds Ratios

To extend the concept of odds ratio to general contingency tables, the techniques described in Chapter 2 Sections A or B and Chapter 3 Section A must be combined. Even if the variables are not binary, the set of variables forming the table can be divided into two exclusive and exhaustive groups. By fixing a joint category of the variables in the second group (that is, a marginal cell in their marginal table), the conditional distribution of the rest of the variables can be considered. This is best described by a contingency table formed by the variables in the first group and containing only those observations that fall into the fixed joint category of the variables in the second group. Any odds ratio in this contingency table is a conditional odds ratio of the first group of variables, given the fixed joint category of the variables in the second set. This is the approach described in Chapter 3 Section A. When this conditional table is not binary—that is, some of the variables have more than two categories—the odds ratios in this table (which are the conditional odds ratios in the original table) can be defined by an appropriate generalization of the local odds ratios (see Chapter 2 Section A) or of the spanning cell odds ratios (see Chapter 2 Section B). Either one of these generalizations can be carried out by confining attention to the table formed by the first set of variables. The number (including the possibility of this number being 0) or other attributes of the conditioning variables (i.e., the variables in the second set) are of no importance.

To illustrate the general concept of odds ratio for contingency tables, yet another form of the World War II American Soldiers data is given in Table 4.1. This is a four-dimensional contingency table, with the variables

TABLE 4.1

Preferred Camp Location of World War II American Soldiers
Cross-Classified by Location of the Present Camp,
Region of Origin, and Race

Race	Region	Location	Prefer to Stay	Prefer to Move			Undecided
				North	South	Undecided	
Black	North	North	196	191	36	41	52
		South	83	875	167	153	111
	South	North	261	122	270	113	105
		South	924	381	788	353	272
White	North	North	367	588	162	191	162
		South	346	874	164	273	164
	South	North	54	50	176	40	40
		South	481	91	389	91	91

SOURCE: Stouffer et al. (1949).

Preference, Location, Region of Origin, and Race. Here Preference has five categories, just as in Table 2.2, which is a marginal of Table 4.1. A simplified version of the data in Table 4.1 was given in Table 3.4, in which the last two (undecided) categories of the variable Preference were removed and the remaining three categories were recoded into two.

If, for example, the goal of the analysis is to compare the relationships among Region, Location, and Preference for black and white soldiers, the first group of variables will consist of Region, Location, and Preference; the second group will contain the variable Race only. Conditioning on the category Black results in the upper half of Table 4.1; conditioning on the category White results in the lower half of Table 4.1. One can analyze both conditional tables similarly, but the analyses can be carried out independently.

The conditional tables considered above are three-dimensional. If they were binary, the second-order odds ratio in Equation 3.3 could be used to measure the amount of association. In the present case, when the variables are not (all) binary, several 2^3 subtables can be defined and the odds ratios in each of these subtables calculated. The categories of every polytomous variable must be divided into adjacent pairs as the first and second, second and third, and so on. If a variable is binary (i.e., dichotomous), we have only one pair of categories. In the example, the variables Region and Location are binary, with categories North and South, and Preference has five categories, denoted as PSt, PN, PS, PU, and U. The categories of the three variables give 1, 1, and 4 adjacent pairs, respectively, and they define $1 \times 1 \times 4 = 4$ subtables of size 2^3. These are as follows: $(N, S) \times (N, S) \times (PSt, PN)$, $(N, S) \times (N, S) \times (PN, PS)$, $(N, S) \times (N, S) \times (PS, PU)$, and $(N, S) \times (N, S) \times (PU, U)$. The odds ratios in these subtables are the local odds ratios in the conditional table. For black soldiers, the first one of these is

$$\frac{f_{1111} f_{1122} f_{1212} f_{1221}}{f_{1222} f_{1211} f_{1121} f_{1112}} \qquad [4.1]$$

and the second one is

$$\frac{f_{1112} f_{1123} f_{1213} f_{1222}}{f_{1223} f_{1212} f_{1122} f_{1113}} \qquad [4.2]$$

The numerical values of the four conditional local odds ratios for black soldiers are 12.26, 1.08, 0.75, and 0.69. These conditional local odds ratios measure the amount of association that cannot be attributed to a subset of the variables, conditionally on the fixed category (or categories) of the conditioning variable (or variables). Because some of the values of the local conditional odds ratios are far from 1, one can conclude that, in the relevant parts of the table, there is second-order association among the variables Region, Location, and Preference for black soldiers. Recall from Chapter 3 that Equation 4.1 is the ratio of the conditional odds ratios of Location and Preference conditioned on Race = Black, and on Region = North in the numerator and Region = South in the denominator. Therefore, we have found that for black soldiers whose region of origin is in the North, the association among Location and their wish to stay in their present camps—as opposed to moving to a(nother) camp in the North—is about 12 times as strong as it is for black soldiers from the South.

When the conditional odds ratios are computed for white soldiers, we must change the index of Race, that is, the first index. The following values are obtained: 7.72, 0.56, 1.37, and 0.71. From these figures, one sees immediately that the preference to stay in Northern camps is nearly eight times as strong for white soldiers from the North as for white soldiers from the South, but generally the effect of Region is weaker for white soldiers than for black soldiers because the conditional odds ratios are closer to 1.

When association between Location and Preference is of interest, one has to consider the conditional odds ratio of these two variables given any combination of Race and Region. In this case, the conditional tables are 2×5 and there are four conditional tables. In every conditional table we have $1 \times 4 = 4$ local odds ratios. For example, the first local conditional

TABLE 4.2
Conditional Spanning Cell Odds Ratios of the Data in Table 4.1
Conditioned on Race With Spanning Cell (1, 1, 1)

Condition	Spanning Cell			
	(2, 2, 2)	(2, 2, 3)	(2, 2, 4)	(2, 2, 5)
Black	12.26	13.29	9.99	6.89
White	7.72	4.33	5.94	4.20

odds ratio, that is, the one computed from categories PSt and PN of Preference, for Region = North and Race = Black, is 10.82 and the same quantity for Region = South and Race = Black is 0.88. These quantities are the direct measures of persistence to the North for the two groups of black soldiers. The ratio of these two values, as was calculated above, is 12.26 (except for rounding error). From this one sees that persistence to the North is much stronger for black soldier from the North than for black soldiers from the South. In addition, out of the two effects compared, one shows a strong persistence to a location in the North, whereas the other shows a slight dispreference.

The generalization of spanning cell odds ratios to higher dimensional tables is simpler than the generalization of local odds ratios. -f the indices of every variable are different in two cells, then these cells span a binary contingency table. Therefore, if the cell with all indices equal to 1 is selected as the reference cell, any cell that does not contain the index 1 can serve as a spanning cell. The odds ratio in the binary table defined by the reference cell and a spanning cell is computed as in Chapter 3. When both the reference cell and the spanning cell are selected from a conditional table, the odds ratio is a conditional odds ratio. Conditioned on Race, there are $1 \times 1 \times 4 = 4$ spanning cell odds ratios. When the reference cell is cell (1, 1, 1), the conditional odds ratio, for black soldiers, belonging to the spanning cell (2, 2, 2) is 12.26. The same conditional spanning cell odds ratio for white soldiers is 7.72. These figures are the same as the first local conditional odds ratios. The values of the other spanning cell conditional odds ratios differ from the values of the local conditional odds ratios. The two sets of odds ratios are related by rules similar to those given in Chapter 2 Section B. The conditional spanning cell odds ratios for the data in Table 4.1 are given in Table 4.2.

The spanning cell odds ratios measure how strong the association is among Region, Location, and Preference, conditioned on one of the categories of

Race, if Preference is a binary variable, with one of the categories being preference to stay, and the other category is defined by the spanning cell, that is, PN, PS, PU, U, respectively. We see that the strongest conditional association among Region, Location, and Preference is obtained when Preference is restricted to categories PSt and PS. This association is very strong for black soldiers and weaker, but still strong, for white soldiers. Note, however, that all spanning cell odds ratios are substantially greater than 1, showing that the association between Location and Preference is stronger for soldiers whose region of origin is in the North than for those from the South (for both black and white soldiers). That is, the ratio of the odds of preferring to stay in their present camp (as opposed to wishing to move to another location or being undecided) for soldiers who are in the North to the same odds for soldiers who are presently in the South is greater for soldiers who came from the North than for soldiers who came from the South. This remains true when the preference for staying in the present camp is compared to any other category of Preference.

More generally, for a five-dimensional table, the variables may be divided into two sets and the conditional odds ratio of the variables in the first set, given a joint category of the variables in the second set, may be considered. If the variables in the first set have I, J, and K categories, respectively, and the variables in the second set have L and M categories, respectively (that is, there are three variables in the first set and two variables in the second one), there are LM conditional tables. In each of these, there are $(I-1)(J-1)(K-1)$ local, or spanning cell, odds ratios. Combined, there are $(I-1)(J-1)(K-1)LM$ conditional odds ratios in this case. Every one of these pertains to a specific combination of the categories of the two conditioning variables and measures association among the other three variables in a specific part of the table, association that cannot be attributed to any subset of them. Just like in the case of lower-dimensional tables, *any* conditional odds ratio can be expressed as a function of the conditional local odds ratios or of the conditional spanning cell odds ratios.

When the second set of variables is empty, there is no variable to condition on, and 1 obtains the odds ratio of the variables forming the table. The order of this is 1 less than the number of variables forming the table.

B. Mixed Parameterization of the Cell Probabilities

It was shown in the previous section that, for example, for a five-dimensional $I \times J \times K \times L \times M$ table conditioned on the last two variables, there are $(I-1)(J-1)(K-1)LM$ conditional odds ratios (local or spanning cell). To parameterize the $I \times J \times K \times L \times M$ table, one needs $IJKLM - 1$ parameters (the last one is obtained from the fact that the probabilities add up to 1, or the observed frequencies sum to the sample size). The collection of conditional odds ratios can be completed with certain marginal probabilities to obtain a parameterization of the distribution in the table.

It remains true in the generality considered here that *conditional odds ratios are always defined on an ascending system of subsets of variables* and *marginal distributions are always defined on a descending system of subsets of variables.* The second statement is obvious; the first one is true because the same result was true for binary tables, and the odds ratios here are defined as a collection of odds ratios for binary tables. The result that the complement of an ascending system is descending, and vice versa, does not depend on any property of the variables; therefore, it remains true.

If the five variables are denoted by A, B, C, D, and E, then in the above example the conditional odds ratios are given for ABC conditioned on D and E. Consequently, the conditional odds ratios are also given for $ABCD$, conditioned on E, for $ABCE$, conditioned on D, and for $ABCDE$. These are the subsets contained in the ascending system generated by ABC. The complement of this ascending system is a descending system, where the maximal subsets are $ABDE$, $ACDE$, and $BCDE$, that is, all four-variable subsets, except for those that contain ABC as a subset. These two classes are illustrated below, with subsets in the ascending class overlined and subsets in the descending class underlined.

$$\overline{ABCDE}$$
$$\overline{ABCD}, \overline{ABCE}, \underline{ABDE}, \underline{ACDE}, \underline{BCDE}$$
$$\overline{ABC}, \underline{ABD}, \underline{ABE}, \underline{ACD}, \underline{ACE}, \underline{ADE}, \underline{BCD}, \underline{BCE}, \underline{BDE}, \underline{CDE}$$
$$\underline{AB}, \underline{AC}, \underline{AD}, \underline{AE}, \underline{BC}, \underline{BD}, \underline{BE}, \underline{CD}, \underline{CE}, \underline{DE}$$
$$\underline{A}, \underline{B}, \underline{C}, \underline{D}, \underline{E}$$
$$\underline{\varnothing}$$

Out of the three maximal subsets in the descending system, the marginal distribution of $ABDE$ contains $IJLM - 1$ parameters. The marginal of $ACDE$ contains $ILM(K-1)$ new parameters ($K-1$ parameters, as the conditional distribution of C, in every joint category of A, D, and E). The marginal of $BCDE$ contains, as the marginals BDE and CDE are already given, $LM(J-1)(K-1)$ additional parameters. To see this, consider the $BCDE$ marginal, as the combination of the DE marginal with the conditional distribution of BC. This conditional distribution is needed for every joint category of *DE,* that is, *LM* times. If a joint category of *D* and *E* is fixed, then the conditional distributions of *B* and *C* also are given from the *BDE* and *CDE* marginals. Therefore, one only needs to compute the number of new parameters needed to define the joint conditional distribution of *B* and *C,* and this is $(J-1)(K-1)$.

Combining the numbers of parameters associated with the conditional odds ratios on the ascending system and with the marginal distributions on the complement descending system, one obtains that $(I-1)(J-1)(K-1)LM + IJLM - 1 + ILM(K-1) + LM(J-1)(K-1) = IJKLM - JKLM - IKLM - IJLM + KLM + JLM + ILM - LM + IJLM - 1 + IKLM - ILM + JKLM - KLM - JLM + LM = IJKLM - 1$, that is, the desired number of parameters in a $I \times J \times K \times L \times M$ table.

The conditional odds ratios on an ascending system and the marginal distributions on the complement descending system not only parameterize the distribution but also are also variation independent.

Variation independence implies that the conditional odds ratios, whether local or spanning cell, are the proper measures of association in the conditional tables because they contain all the information in the conditional distributions that cannot be attributed to smaller subsets and depend only on this information. When the values of the conditional odds ratios are used to analyze a distribution, the variables are divided into two groups. The association among the variables in the first group is described by the collection of local, or spanning cell, odds ratios; the effects of the variables in the second group are removed by holding these variables constant. Their effect, however, shows in the differences in the conditional associations depending on the joint category of the conditioning variables where the odds ratios of the other variables are computed.

C. Log-Linear and Other Association Models

In this section, various statistical models will be defined as restrictions on the odds ratios of a contingency table. Several of the widely used techniques are aimed at modeling the association structure of the distribution and, consequently, assume a "simple" structure of appropriate collections of conditional odds ratios. The simple structure can be prescribed values, or a prescribed pattern, or a prescribed functional form of the conditional odds ratios.

The first case to be considered is when values of the conditional odds ratios are prescribed. The prescribed values can be taken from either theoretical considerations or from previous observations. The extension of the conditional odds ratios from a subset to a subset containing one more variable is the ratio of two appropriate conditional odds ratios. Therefore, *if all the prescribed values of the conditional odds ratios are 1, then all other odds ratios on the generated ascending system will also be equal to 1.* Recall that if the conditional odds ratio of a subset of variables is 1, then these variables have no conditional association that could not be attributed to some of their subsets (given the categories of the other variables). Therefore, the above statement is equivalent to saying that *if the lack of conditional associations among the variables in certain subsets of the variables (given the categories of the complement variables) is assumed, then this implies the lack of conditional association among the variables in any subset containing some of the original subsets (given the categories of the respective complement variables).* This lack of conditional association is an ascending property.

If a set contains only two variables, then the lack of conditional association is equivalent to conditional independence. If there are more than two variables in the subset, then conditional independence implies the lack of conditional association, but the lack of conditional association does not imply conditional independence. For example, with three variables conditioned on the other variables, the conditional second-order odds ratio may be equal to 1, even if these three variables are not conditionally independent, given the other variables.

Models assuming the lack of conditional associations within certain sets of variables are usually called *log-linear models.* The lack of conditional association is assumed for subsets in an ascending system. The subsets belonging to the complement descending system are called *interactions,* or allowed interactions, because the lack of conditional associations is not assumed to hold for these subsets. The explanation and interpretation of log-linear models given in Chapter 3 Section C applies here as well. The maximum likelihood estimate under a log-linear model is a distribution that combines the prescribed conditional odds ratios (all equal to 1) with the observed marginal distributions of the subsets in the complement descending system. The maximal subsets in the descending class are sometimes called "fitted marginals" or "maximal interactions." Usually, these are listed to define a log-linear model.

Log-linear models are very useful tools in the analysis of multidimensional contingency tables but, unfortunately, no log-linear model appears to give an adequate description of the data in Table 4.1. The condensed form of these data, given in Table 3.3, was analyzed by several authors.

Goodman (1972) found that the log-linear model with the following maximal interactions fits the data quite well: Race, Region, Location; Race, Preference; and Region, Location, Preference. For the data in Table 4.1, this model yields a Pearson chi-squared statistic of 237.53, on 12 degrees of freedom, indicating a very poor fit. Another model, which Goodman (1972) found an adequate description of the data in the form given in Table 3.3, contains the following maximal interactions: Race, Region, Location; Race, Region, Preference; and Region, Location, Preference. For the data in the form given in Table 4.1, this model yields a Pearson chi-squared statistic of 194.30, on 8 degrees of freedom, suggesting that this model is very far from being an adequate description of the data or of the underlying population.

The log-linear model that assumes only that the third-order odds ratio (of all four variables) is equal to 1 still shows a poor fit: The Pearson chi-squared statistic is 11.83, on 4 degrees of freedom. The tail probability of the reference distribution is less than 0.02. In this model, all four subsets consisting of three variables are allowed interactions, and these are the maximal ones. This model can be interpreted as all three explanatory variables (Race, Region, Location) having effects on Preference; moreover, every pair of these explanatory variables has a joint effect that cannot be attributed to any one of these variables. There is, however, no joint effect of the three explanatory variables on Preference.

The model considered above is the least restrictive possible log-linear model for a four-way table. It assumes that the third-order odds ratio is equal to 1. Because one of the variables is not binary, but has five categories, the third-order odds ratio is a collection of four numbers that the model assumes are equal to 1. From the point of view of data description, this model is too restrictive because it sets four parameters equal to 1 at the same time.

Log-linear models set all values of certain conditional odds ratios equal to 1 at the same time. More flexible models prescribe the values of some of the conditional odds ratios to values other than 1. These are prescribed conditional association, or generalized log-linear, models. Note that when the odds ratio is assumed to be equal to 1, this applies equally to local or spanning cell odds ratios. When values different from 1 are assumed, the models take on different forms depending on whether the values of the local or of spanning cell odds ratios are prescribed. The fit of the log-linear model, which assumes that the values of the third-order odds ratios are all equal to 1, can be greatly improved if, instead of 1, the common value of the spanning cell odds ratios is assumed to be equal to 2. For this model, one obtains a Pearson chi-squared statistic of 4.90, on 4 degrees of freedom; the tail probability of the reference distribution is 0.30. One should not conclude, however, that this model is a good description of the population underlying the data. The model is a good description of the data, but this does not mean that we should believe that the model describes the population as well. This conclusion could only be justified if theoretical considerations or previous experience strongly suggested a model and the data did not seem to contradict it. When, instead of testing a pre-defined model, one uses the data to govern a model-building or a model-finding procedure, acceptable fit, in itself, does not imply that the model could be considered an adequate description of the underlying population. This applies to any statistical model, not just those considered here. Data-driven model-building procedures are, however, important exploratory tools, and finding a model with the prescribed values of some of the conditional odds ratios that describes the data well may give insight regarding the association structure among the variables.

For analyses where theoretical considerations or previous knowledge leads to prescribed conditional association models, see Rudas and Leimer (1992), where technical details of the fitting procedure also are given. Prescribed conditional association models can be fitted, among other programs, by the *MixLInMult* module of the DISTAN package (Rudas, 1992).

In Chapter 2, association models were considered for two-dimensional tables that prescribed not values but rather a certain "simple" structure, or pattern, of the local or the spanning cell odds ratios. Similar models can be defined for higher-dimensional tables as well. The definition of these association models was based on the fact that, for an $I \times J$ table, both the local and the spanning cell odds ratios can be arranged in an $(I - 1) \times (J - 1)$ table where the models assumed a certain simple pattern, such as row effects only. For higher dimensional tables, the local or spanning cell odds ratios can also be arranged in the form of a rectangular table. For a three-dimensional $I \times J \times K$ table, the second order odds ratio of the three variables is a collection of second order odds ratios that pertain to small $2 \times 2 \times 2$ tables. There are $(I - 1)(J - 1)(K - 1)$ local $2 \times 2 \times 2$ tables, which can be naturally arranged into an $(I - 1) \times (J - 1) \times (K - 1)$ rectangular array. The second order local odds ratios can be arranged the same way. For spanning cell odds ratios, using cell $(1, 1, 1)$ as the reference cell, there is one second order odds ratio that belongs to every cell that does not have an index equal to 1. These cells are in an $(I - 1) \times (J - 1) \times (K - 1)$ part of the original table.

Conditional odds ratios also can be arranged in a rectangular array. If there are five variables, for example, and the conditional odds ratios of the first three are considered at a fixed joint category of the last two variables, the conditional table is three dimensional and the odds ratios have the same structure as described in the above paragraph. If the last two variables have L and M categories, respectively, then one obtains LM of these $(i - 1) \times (J - 1) \times (K - 1)$ tables.

One can define association models by assuming a simple structure, or pattern, of the rectangular arrays containing the conditional local or spanning cell odds ratios. In the case of a five-dimensional table, for example, when the conditional odds ratio of the first three variables is considered, given the last two variables, the conditional odds ratios can be written in the form α_{lm}^{ijk}, where the subscripts refer to the categories of the conditioning variables and the superscripts identify the position of the odds ratios. For both local and spanning cell odds ratios, i may be selected as the greater index for the first variable in the relevant subtable, j as the greater index of the second variable, and k as the greater index of the third variable. With this choice of indices, $i = 2, \ldots, I, j = 2, \ldots, J, k = 2, \ldots, K$ for both local and spanning cell odds ratios. Various assumptions are possible as to how α_{lm}^{ijk} depends on the indices i, j, k, l, m. For example, the assumption

$$\alpha_{lm}^{ijk} = f(i) \qquad [4.3]$$

says that the conditional odds ratios depend on i only and not on the other two indices nor the conditioning variables. Assuming

$$\alpha_{lm}^{ijk} = g(i)h(m) \qquad [4.4]$$

amounts to saying that the conditional odds ratios depend on i and on one of the conditioning variables, through the index m only, and that these two effects influence the conditional odds ratios independently from each other. Or, assuming

$$\alpha_{lm}^{ijk} = t(i, m)u(j, k, l) \qquad [4.5]$$

means that the conditional odds ratios are influenced by two independent factors. One is the interaction between the first and fifth variables, and the other is the interaction among the second, third, and fourth variables. In general, the $(I - 1) \times (J - 1) \times (K - 1) \times L \times M$ array of conditional odds ratios can be analyzed by any linear (that is, additive) or log-linear (i.e., multiplicative) model.

At present, little experience is available regarding the application of these general association models. However, Chapter 6 of Clogg and Shihadeh (1994) considers conditional association models for three-way tables.

Log-linear, generalized log-linear, and association models all can be given a unified formulation in terms of restrictions on some of the conditional odds ratios, but such a general approach lies outside the scope of this book. There is, however, one more generalization, which leads to a widely used class of models.

If, in the above example, the conditioning variables (i.e., the fourth and fifth variables) are assumed to be numerical rather than categorical, one may assume that the conditional odds ratios are linear functions of the values l and m of the last two variables. These models lead to *logistic regression* in a general form:

$$\alpha_{lm}^{ijk} = exp(\gamma_{ijk} l + \delta_{ijk} m + \varepsilon_{ijk}) \qquad [4.6]$$

where the γ_{ijk}, δ_{ijk}, ε_{ijk} coefficients depend on categories i, j, and k. More restricted models may assume that some of the coefficients do not depend on all three indices. In their traditional form, logistic regression models describe the odds pertaining to one variable only, rather than odds ratios pertaining to several variables. The assumption that the logarithm of the odds (or of the odds ratio) is described by a linear function is traditional and could be replaced by any other class of functions. See DeMaris (1992), Liao (1994), and Menard (1995) for more detailed accounts of logistic regression and related models.

D. Log-Linear Parameters and Conditional Odds Ratios

As was pointed out in Chapter 3 Section C, log-linear models are usually defined by assuming that the log-linear parameters pertaining to an ascending class of subsets of the variables forming the contingency table are equal to 0. Log-linear parameters in the general case are defined similarly to the definitions applied to special cases earlier in this book. The log-linear parameters can be of the λ or μ type. The λ parameters measure effects in terms of deviation from average, and μ parameters measure effects in terms of deviation from a reference cell.

It already has been seen in various setups that all the conditional odds ratios pertaining to an ascending class of subsets of the variables forming the contingency table are equal to 1 if, and only if, the log-linear parameters pertaining to the same ascending system are equal to 0. This result holds in the generality considered here as well. This means that the null, or no-association, value of the conditional odds ratios (i.e., 1) is obtained exactly when the no-interaction value of the log-linear parameters (i.e., 0) is obtained. Lack of conditional association and lack of log-linear interaction are identical for an ascending system of the variables forming the table.

The relationship between log-linear parameters and conditional odds ratios is, however, stronger than what is indicated by the above results. They are one-to-one functions of one another whether they indicate the lack or the presence of association. The exact formulas that can be used to convert log-linear parameters into conditional odds ratios and vice versa can also be used to convert λ- and μ-type log-linear parameters into each other (see Leimer & Rudas, 1989). Here only the formulas to convert spanning cell conditional odds ratios into μ-type log-linear parameters, and vice versa, will be dealt with. The formulas for λ log-linear parameters and/or local conditional odds ratios are more complicated.

In the case of variables A, B, C, and D, for example, a spanning cell conditional odds ratio of the last three variables, given a category of the first one, can be written as $COR(B, C, D, (j', k', l')| A = i)$, where i is the category of the conditioning variable and (j', k', l') is a spanning cell for the variables B, C, D. Denoting the μ log-linear parameter for the BCD interaction in cell (j', k', l') by $\mu_{j'k'l'}^{BCD}$,

$$\mu_{j'k'l'}^{BCD} = -log(COR(B, C, D, (j', k', l')|A = 1)) \qquad [4.6]$$

and

$$\mu_{ij'k'l'}^{ABCD} = log(COR(B, C, D, (j', k', l')|A = 1)) \qquad [4.7]$$

$$-log(COR(B, C, D, (j', k', l')|A = i'))$$

Note that the μ log-linear parameters are 0 in every cell that is not a spanning cell for the subset of variables to which the parameter pertains. Using the above formulae and the conditional odds ratios given in Table 4.2, we can compute the μ log-linear parameters on the relevant ascending class for the data in Table 4.1. In the application of the above formulae, A = Race, B = Region, C = Location, and D = Preference; the first category of A is Black, and i' can only take on the value of 2, which is White. Similarly, j' and k' can only be South, and l' can take on four values, or categories. The results are given in Table 4.3.

TABLE 4.3
μ Log-linear Parameters for the Data in Table 4.1
for Selected Interactions

a. *Region, Location, and Preference*

Race	Region	Location	Prefer to Stay	Prefer to Move			Undecided
				North	South	Undecided	
Black	North	North	0	0	0	0	0
		South	0	0	0	0	0
	South	North	0	0	0	0	0
		South	0	−2.50	−2.59	−2.30	−1.93
White	North	North	0	0	0	0	0
		South	0	0	0	0	0
	South	North	0	0	0	0	0
		South	0	−2.50	−2.59	−2.30	−1.93

b. *Race, Region, Location, and Preference*

Race	Region	Location	Prefer to Stay	Prefer to Move			Undecided
				North	South	Undecided	
Black	North	North	0	0	0	0	0
		South	0	0	0	0	0
	South	North	0	0	0	0	0
		South	0	0	0	0	0
White	North	North	0	0	0	0	0
		South	0	0	0	0	0
	South	North	0	0	0	0	0
		South	0	0.460	1.12	0.52	0.5

In this simple example, the formula to convert μ log-linear parameters into conditional odds ratios is equivalent to Equation 4.6. The more general formula for larger tables and other subsets is given in Leimer and Rudas (1989).

5. CONCLUSIONS

The present monograph intends to give a unified treatment to several methods for the analysis of contingency tables through the study of conditional odds ratios. For the reader unfamiliar with these methods, it gives a solid basis, and encouragement, for the further study of log-linear and other association models. For the reader who has already studied these methods in other texts, it gives a review of some of the most important common features and helps to understand how these methods are related to each other.

The main line of argument in this book is that higher-order conditional odds ratios are variation independent from lower-order marginals, and therefore they are natural measures of association. Association, in this approach, is defined as the information in a higher-order joint distribution that is not present in lower-order marginals. Conditional odds ratios extend naturally to ascending systems of subsets of variables, whereas the marginal distributions extend naturally to descending systems. Together, these two sets of parameters give a meaningful parameterization of the joint distribution. Several models can be obtained by applying restrictions on the conditional odds ratios. When these are assumed to be equal to 1 (on an ascending system), one obtains log-linear models; when they have other prescribed values, one obtains generalized log-linear, or prescribed conditional interaction, models. Other models assume that the conditional odds ratios have a specified pattern (association models) or that they are specified functions of other parameters (including logistic regression models).

I have largely omitted problems related to fitting and testing of these models. Only the iterative proportional fitting procedure was described. This not only yields the maximum likelihood estimates under log-linear and generalized log-linear models but has theoretical importance as well. The other models referred to in this book require different methods for the computation of maximum likelihood estimates. While estimation is done almost exclusively by commercial packages and the user can be quite confident regarding the reliability of these, testing raises different problems and very often requires judgment by the researchers.

Both "small" and "large" sample sizes may cause problems, and there are no clear-cut criteria available for deciding whether the actual sample warrants worrying about any of the undesirable effects. With small samples, the percentage points of the reference distribution are not valid in the sense that they lead to tests with levels different from the nominal level. There is a huge literature on how different statistics behave under small sample sizes. For an overview, see Read and Cressie (1988). In a comparison of the two most widely used statistics, the Pearson chi-squared and the likelihood ratio, I found (Rudas, 1986) that with small samples the Pearson chi-squared statistic is more appropriate, but the literature on this issue is not conclusive.

In the case of large samples, one has different problems, mainly related to the fact that most testing methods test for *statistical significance,* but the researcher is more interested in *subject matter significance.* With large samples, these two concepts tend to be very different. An alternative approach to measuring the fit of a statistical model that is able to distinguish between statistical significance (effect in the sample of a magnitude that is not likely to be the result of sampling) and subject matter significance (the presence of an effect in the population that is larger than the magnitude of possible measurement error) was put forward in Rudas, Clogg, and Lindsay (1994) and Clogg, Rudas, and Xi (1995).

REFERENCES

AGRESTI, A. (1990) *Categorical Data Analysis.* New York: John Wiley.

BISHOP, Y. M. M., FIENBERG, S. E., and HOLLAND, P. W. (1975) *Discrete Multivariate Analysis: Theory and Practice.* Cambridge: M.I.T. Press.

CLOGG, C. C., RUDAS, T., and XI, L. (1995) "A new index of structure for the analysis of models for mobility tables and other cross-classifications," in P. Marsden (Ed.), *Sociological Methodology* 1995 (pp. 197-222). Oxford, UK: Blackwell.

CLOGG, C. C., and SHIHADEH, E. S. (1994) *Statistical Models for Ordinal Variables.* Thousand Oaks, CA: Sage.

DARROCH, J. N., LAURITZEN, S. L., and SPEED, T. P. (1980) "Markov fields and log-linear models for contingency tables." *Annals of Statistics* 8: 522-539.

DeMARIS, A. (1992) *Logit Modeling.* Sage University Papers Series on Quantitative Applications in the Social Sciences, 07-086. Thousand Oaks, CA: Sage.

DIXON, W. J. (1981) *BMDP Statistical Software.* Los Angeles: UCLA Press.

ELIASON, S. R. (1993) *Maximum Likelihood Estimation: Logic and Practice.* Sage University Papers Series on Quantitative Applications in the Social Sciences, 07-096. Thousand Oaks, CA: Sage.

GOKHALE, D. V., and KULLBACK, S. (1978) *The Information in Contingency Tables.* New York: Marcel Dekker.

GOODMAN, L. A. (1972) "A modified multiple regression approach to the analysis of dichotomous variables." *American Sociological Review* 37: 28-46.

HABERMAN, S. J. (1974) *The Analysis of Frequency Data.* Chicago: The University of Chicago Press.

HAGENAARS, J. A. (1993) *Loglinear Models With Latent Variables.* Sage University Papers Series on Quantitative Applications in the Social Sciences, 07-094. Thousand Oaks, CA: Sage.

ISHII-KUNTZ, M. (1994) *Ordinal Log-Linear Models.* Sage University Papers Series on Quantitative Applications in the Social Sciences, 07-097. Thousand Oaks, CA: Sage.

KNOKE, D., and BURKE, P. J. (1980) *Log-Linear Models.* Sage University Papers Series on Quantitative Applications in the Social Sciences, 07-020. Beverly Hills, CA: Sage.

LEIMER, H.-G., and RUDAS, T. (1989) "Conversion between GLIM- and BMDP-type log-linear parameters." *GLIM Newsletter* 19: 47.

LIAO, T. F. (1994) *Interpreting Probability Models: Logit, Probit, and Other Generalized Linear Models.* Sage University Papers Series on Quantitative Applications in the Social Sciences, 07-101. Thousand Oaks, CA: Sage.

MENARD, S. (1995) *Applied Logistic Regression.* Sage University Papers Series on Quantitative Applications in the Social Sciences 07-106. Thousand Oaks, CA: Sage.

NORUSIS, M. J. (1994) *SPSS Advanced Statistics 6.1.* Chicago: SPSS Inc.

PAYNE, C. (Ed.) (1986) *The GLIM System Manual.* Oxford, UK: NAG.

READ, T. R. C., and CRESSIE, N. A. C. (1988) *Goodness-of-Fit Statistics for Discrete Multivariate Data.* New York: Springer.

REYNOLDS, H. T. (1984) *Analysis of Nominal Data* (2nd ed.) Sage University Papers Series on Quantitative Applications in the Social Sciences, 07-007. Thousand Oaks, CA: Sage.

RUDAS, T. (1986) "A Monte Carlo comparison of the small sample behaviour of the Pearson, the likelihood ratio, and the Cressie-Read statistics." *Journal of Statistical Computation and Simulation* 24: 107-120.

RUDAS, T. (1991) "Prescribed conditional interaction structure models with application to the analysis of mobility tables." *Quality and Quantity* 25: 345-358.

RUDAS, T. (1992) *DISTAN 2.0 Manual,* Budapest: TÁRKI.

RUDAS, T., CLOGG, C. C., and LINDSAY, B. G. (1994) "A new index of fit based on mixture methods for the analysis of contingency tables." *Journal of the Royal Statistical Society* Ser B 56: 623-639.

RUDAS, T., and LEIMER, H.-G. (1992) "Analysis of contingency tables with known conditional odds ratios or known log-linear parameters" in P. G. Van Der Heijden et al. (Eds.), *Statistical Modeling*. Amsterdam: Elsevier.

STOUFFER, S. A., SUCHMANN, E. A., DEVINNEY, L. C., STAR S. A., and WILLIAMS, R. M. (1949) *The American Soldier* (Vol. 1). Princeton, NJ: Princeton University Press.

WHITTAKER, J. (1990) *Graphical Models in Applied Multivariate Analysis*. New York: John Wiley.

ABOUT THE AUTHOR

TAMÁS RUDAS has a doctorate in mathematics from the Eötvös University and currently is the Head of the Center for Applied Statistics at the Central European University. He is also affiliated with the Social Science Informatics Center (TÁRKI). Previously, he was Reader and Head in the Statistics Group of the Institute of Sociology of the Eötvös University, and he has held visiting positions with the Pennsylvania State Univertsity, the University of Toledo, and the Educational Testing Service. His main research interest lies in methods for categorical data analysis. He has published papers in statistics and social science methodology journals, including the *Journal of the Royal Statistical Society, Journal of Educational and Behavioral Statistics, Sociological Methodology,* and *Quality and Quantity.*